COUPLES THERAPY WORKBOOK

HOW TO RECONNECT WITH YOUR PARTNER THROUGH HONEST COMMUNICATION. OVERCOME THE ANXIETY IN RELATIONSHIP AND BUILD A STRONG EMOTIONAL INTIMACY LAYING THE FOUNDATIONS FOR UNCONDITIONAL LOVE

THERESA MILLER

Congratulation on purchase this Book and thank You for doing so

Please enjoy!

THERESA MILLER is a cognitive therapist focusing on the treatment of anxiety and addiction, committed to studying and researching methods to complement therapy - a line of work she continues to pursue successfully among her patients.

She is particularly interested in affective vulnerability factors, such as distress intolerance and attachment, that are common across psychological disorders, with a focus on those that can be modified with behavioral treatment.

Other focus are on the behavioral therapies then, also if are highly effective for a number of psychiatric disorders, there is significant room for improvement, in generally.

His first work, now published over one year ago, was "Best Seller" in the Anxiety Disorder category for many time, but it is advisable to have it also in the audiobook version.

Her passion is to help adults and teenager, helping them to achieve a better quality of life by confronting issues of depression, anxiety, stress, and low self-esteem, shown their how to use their mind to detox.

THERESA MILLER is an impact maker who aspires to bring out the best in everyone she comes in contact with.

Follow her for more and new updates on fb →

https://www.facebook.com/theresamiller.author

No part of this publication may be reproduced, distributed, or transmitted in any form or by any means, including photocopying, recording, or other electronic or mechanical methods, or by any information storage and retrieval system without the prior written permission of the publisher, except in the case of very brief quotations embodied in critical reviews and certain other noncommercial uses permitted by copyright law.

∼

© Copyright 2020 by **THERESA MILLER**
All rights reserved

I can assure you that these topics were carefully chosen to include several difficulties in marriage. I hope that you not only read this book, but also deeply understand the lessons and their importance in helping your relationship grow better and become warmer, stronger, and healthier. I am convinced that when you put this knowledge into action, you would experience your marriage blossoming and grow into the beautiful and forever union it was meant to be. It is my wish that you keep falling in love, over and over, again and again, with that same person you married. Your marriage would be beautiful and healthy! So let's begin, shall we?

CONTENTS

1. Topic 1:	1
2. Emotional Intelligence?	2
3. What is Emotional Intelligence?	3
4. Who is an emotionally intelligent person?	5
5. Sample scenario:	9
6. What is emotional un-intelligence?	12
7. Practice exercise	16
Afterword	17
8. Topic 2:	18
9. Poor Communication? What does it mean?	21
10. Communication building Exercise	30
11. Topic 3:	32
12. What is Appreciation? What is Gratitude?	33
13. What lack of appreciation causes	37
14. What are words of affirmation and affection?	39
15. Practical appreciation exercises	43
Afterword	47
16. Topic 4:	48
17. What do I mean by Negotiation?	49
18. What does it mean to compromise?	50
19. Practice Activity:	61
Afterword	63
Your Feedback	65
20. Topic 5:	66
21. Sub-topic 2:	69
22. Sub-topic 3:	74
23. Practice Exercise	80
24. Topic 6:	81
25. Who is a codependent person?	83
Afterword	93
26. Topic 7:	94
27. Quality Time	97
28. Receiving Gifts	99

29. Acts Of Service	101
30. Physical Touch	103
31. Primary and Secondary love languages	105
32. Desire discrepancy	109
33. Practical Exercises	112
Afterword	113
34. Topic 8:	114
35. What are Erotic Blueprints?	115
36. What are the 5 Erotic Blueprints?	116
37. #1. Energetic	117
38. #2. Sensual	118
39. #3. Sexual	119
40. #4. Kinky	120
41. #5. Shapeshifter	121
42. Practice exercise	125
Afterword	127
Afterword	129
43. Topic 1:	130
44. Topic 2:	131
45. Topic 3:	132
46. Topic 4:	133
47. Topic 5:	134
48. Topic 6:	135
49. Topic 7:	136
50. Topic 8:	137
Want More?	139
Review Ask	143

TOPIC 1:

How we connect emotionally

Emotional Intelligence

In every successful and happy marriage, it is important that both partners connect with each other emotionally and are fully aware of each other's feelings and emotional well-being. We all have different personalities and different ways of showing our emotions. Navigating through the various emotions all take tact and intelligence —especially if you hope to have a successful and vibrant marriage. This is where emotional intelligence becomes necessary.

A happy marriage is an emotionally intelligent one, and it involves two partners who are both committed to self-awareness. They also have the capacity and inclination to manage their own emotional state and its effect on their significant other.

2

EMOTIONAL INTELLIGENCE?

There is this humorous quote that says *'A happily married man is one who understands every word that his wife didn't say'*. This is to a large extent very true, and aptly explains the need for emotional intelligence in a marriage.

This brings us to the first question:

3
WHAT IS EMOTIONAL INTELLIGENCE?

You might have heard the term being used around a lot, it is a fairly popular topic. The term first appeared in 1964 after Joel Robert Davitz and Michael Beldoch, wrote a paper on "The Communication of Emotional Meaning". **It however got very popular after Daniel Goleman, a science journalist, wrote a book about it in 1995.**

By definition, emotional intelligence (also known as **emotional quotient** or **EQ**) is the ability to understand, use, and manage your own emotions in positive ways to relieve stress, communicate effectively, empathize with others, overcome challenges and defuse conflict. In simpler words, *it is the ability to understand and accept one's emotions and manage them in ways that enhances one's relationship with others.*

Emotional intelligence entails the following things:

- Being able to correctly recognize your own emotions and those of others.
- Being capable of discerning between different feelings and labeling them appropriately. –You should be able to discern what you are feeling and not just the usual 'happy, angry or sad'. You should be able to tell the deeper emotions too like nostalgic, grief-stricken, jealous,

defensive, defeated, anxious, nervous, self-critical, grateful, and many others.
- Being able to use emotional information to guide your thinking and behavior. –You should be accurately aware of others emotions as well as yours, and use that information to guide the way you communicate, empathize and relate with people.
- Managing or adjusting your emotions to adapt to whatever environment you are in or to achieve your goal(s). –You should be able to manage your negative emotions (such as anger, jealousy, frustration, vengeance) in-order to achieve your goals.

4

WHO IS AN EMOTIONALLY INTELLIGENT PERSON?

You know those people who know how to be a part of a healthy relationship? It just seems so easy for them to be successful in relationships. Their secret? Emotional intelligence. Or you know that friend or relative that just gets you, and understands what you are feeling before you even verbalize it? Yeah, you guessed right, Emotional Intelligence.

An emotionally intelligent person is someone who has the ability to recognize, understand, and manage his or her emotions and the emotions of others.

Emotionally intelligent people have the following characteristics:

- **They are able to identify their own emotions correctly.** They can correctly identify and recognize what emotions they are feeling whether it be anger, vulnerability, disappointment, nostalgic, jealousy, euphoria.
- **They display emotional self-control.** Emotionally intelligent people do not react immediately to tense situations in an angry and confrontational manner or jump into a quick retort, instead they slow themselves and their responses down. They are proactive rather than reactive people.
- **They can recognize emotions in other people.** Emotionally intelligent people are empathetic and so are

able to correctly identify other people's emotions. Daniel Goleman explains that "If you are tuned out of your own emotions, you will be poor at reading them in other people". They also know how not to take those emotions personally. For example, if a spouse seems distant and upset, an emotionally intelligent partner respects that there might be a hundred and one possible reasons for this and doesn't immediately jump to the assumption that there is something wrong with the marriage or themselves.

- **They manage their emotions well.** They know how to soothe themselves when they are upset. They understand the nuances of feelings and are insightful enough to figure out what exactly is going on with them.
- **They use their EQ in making good decisions.** They use their understanding of their emotions to guide their thinking and behavior and invariably make good and healthy decisions for their lives.
- **They take criticisms well.** Emotionally intelligent people are able to handle any complaints and criticisms in a calm manner. Because of their ability to keep their emotions in check, they think clearly and productively. They do not allow their minds to be clouded by their feelings.
- **They apologize easily.** emotionally intelligent people know the power of saying 'I am sorry'. They also know that saying sorry doesn't always mean you are wrong–just that you value your relationship more than your ego. They say it easily during disagreements and when they realize they have hurt someone's feelings.
- **They understand why people behave the way they do.** Emotionally intelligent people are extremely self-aware. They are aware of the motives and intentions behind the things they themselves do. So they recognize that in other people.
- Emotionally intelligent people are able to recognize other people's needs while also taking care of their own.

- They know how to say the "right" thing to get their desired result.
- **They know what they ought not to say.** Emotional intelligence is not just learning what to say, more importantly, it is learning what not to say. You have to be conscious and aware of "How are these words going to come across?" there is a way to say things and express your opinions that will not come off as hostile or demeaning.

Why is emotional intelligence important in a marriage?

- The more emotionally intelligent a couple is the better able they are to understand, respect and honor each other.
- An emotionally intelligent couple's sex life, relationships and overall happiness is far greater than those who lack emotional intelligence.
- An emotionally intelligent spouse understands their significant other's needs, listens to and validates their perspective, and expresses empathy, which leads to a deeper and better connection between them.
- A high emotional intelligence helps individuals to communicate better, and reduces their anxiety and stress.
- Emotionally intelligent couples resolve their conflicts effectively and bounce back from life's challenges far more rapidly than those who are not emotionally intelligent.
- A spouse that lacks emotional intelligence is difficult to live with, causing resentments and frustration in the marriage, which will inevitably lead to divorce

How do you identify your emotional intelligence (EQ) level?

I would need you to answer these questions honestly, to determine your emotional intelligence level

- Do you have difficulties identifying your feelings accurately?

- Are you quick to react without thinking or understanding what is really going on with you?
- Do you have difficulties remaining calm when having a disagreement with anyone, especially your spouse?
- Do you have difficulties finding a way to calm your raging emotions when you realize you are starting to get upset during a disagreement with your spouse?
- When confronted by someone, is it hard to keep your cool and try to understand their concern?
- Do you get upset and defensive often when your partner is talking to you about a problem?
- Do people, especially your spouse, say that you are always misunderstanding them and are aggressive towards their feelings, concerns and thoughts about issues
- Do people, especially your spouse, friends and coworkers, say that they often feel disrespected by you?

If you answered mostly 'No' to all of these questions, then congratulations! You are an emotionally intelligent person and have a high EQ

If you answered mostly 'yes' then I hate to break it to you but you have a low EQ.

I understand that reading through this and coming to the realization that your EQ might be low could make you uncomfortable. It is alright though, don't panic or get mad yourself, everyone is a work in progress. Trust me there are ways to increase your EQ. If you will stick with me and I will show you practical ways to remedy it and boost your emotional intelligence. So take a deep breath, sit comfortably, open up your mind, be willing to change and make necessary amendments. I will be here with you every step of the way.

So shall we? You are ready? Good!

5

SAMPLE SCENARIO:

*L*et's begin by taking a look at the scenario below:
"Oh come on Sandra! Let it go already! You keep bringing up old stuffs that don't matter"

"No, I'm trying to show you that there is a pattern here. You keep repeatedly doing the same wrongs and refuse to change" Sandra explains,

"Why would you be keeping record of grudges? Let bygones be f*cking bygones!" He yells and begins pacing about the kitchen in an agitated manner.

She truly wanted to have a civil conversation with her husband, one where they both listened and sorted out their issues, but it looked like Dave wasn't going to cooperate. Still, she pushed through the conversation, maintaining a calm attitude and making sure to keep her voice calm and low —Yelling wasn't going to solve this.

"I'm not keeping grudges, Dave. Don't you see what I'm pointing out? What you did today is not an isolated event. It's a pattern. You've done it before!" Try as she might, she couldn't keep the frustration out of her tone, allowing it shine through at the last word.

He stops his pacing abruptly and turns sharply towards her, his expression livid "What f*cking pattern are you drawing up? I don't remember this happening before"

"But I do! I do remember you hurting me this same way." She hated that he wasn't even bothering to apologize for this particular event, instead he was focused on proving that this was a one-time thing and that she was lying

"Of course, you would! You have such a great memory!" The sarcasm and animosity heavy in his voice "I shouldn't be surprised since Elephants never forget."

She immediately takes a sharp intake of breath as if she had been punched in the gut "What do you mean by that?" She demands angrily. Every intention to keep her cool was thrown out the window at that moment. "Exactly what I said." He replies nonchalantly,

"Did you just refer to me as an elephant?" That hurt her really deep, the emotional pain causing a physical burn in her chest. He knew she was insecure about her weight. The menacing glint in his eyes showed he did make that comment on purpose in a bid to hurt her and shut her up.

"Make of it what you want."

His uncaring tone shocks her speechless. Angry tears roll down her face, she doesn't try to hide the hurt and disappointment she feels.

"You are just too sensitive," he declares and walks out of the room angrily.

She slides to the floor slowly, propping her back against the wooden paneled wall of the kitchen. Every bit of energy gone, and in its place she feels defeated, tired and overwhelming sadness. What exactly just happened?

A few Seconds later, she hears the front door open and closes, and realizes she's been left home alone. He left? He really left? While she was trying to communicate to him how his bad habits affected her? The rudeness he had shown towards her made her tear up more, the waterworks flowing unhindered. For a long while she sat on the marbled floor. She didn't know when things got this bad. Of course, she had noticed the red flags before they had been married. But she had hoped he would change, that he would listen more and care about other people's emotions and thoughts. But with the years, he got more selfish, insensitive, angry and judge-mental. She knew she couldn't cope anymore. This marriage was affecting her mental health. On most days, he made her feel like she was the overly sensitive one, the problematic one, that she was the one to blame, that she needed to change, that she wasn't smart enough or pretty enough. She had had enough.

She shakingly rises to her feet, grabs a few kitchen towels from atop the cabinet and wipes the tears and snot from her face. She always was a messy crier, her face swollen and red, her breathing uneven and the occasional hiccups.

She was leaving, a divorce was in order.

So looking at the above scenario, I want you to determine which of the parties is Emotional unintelligent —Sandra or Dave?

It's okay if you are not sure of the answer. This subtopic will guide your decision.

6

WHAT IS EMOTIONAL UN-INTELLIGENCE?

It is the same thing as having a low emotional intelligence. It refers to the inability to accurately perceive emotions (in both yourself and others) and to use that information to guide your thinking and actions.

Emotionally unintelligent people have the following characteristics:

- **They do not manage their emotions well.** They lash out at everyone and everything in their path when they are upset. They have no emotional self-control.
- **They have emotional outbursts.** Because they struggle to control their emotions and barely understand what they are feeling, they lash out re-actively. Their emotional outbursts often seem overblown and uncontrollable, and lasts for minutes, even hours.
- **They always have to be 'Right' and 'Correct'.** This person is argumentative and will argue a point to the death while refusing to listen to anyone else's point of view. Even when you provide them with proof that they are wrong, they will argue that your facts are wrong.
- **They do not take criticisms well.** Because of their need to always be right and correct, they don't take criticisms well.

They get upset, defensive and aggressive at the slightest hint of criticism.
- **They are unaware of the impact of their behavior on others.** Not only do they not know how to manage their own emotions, But they also seem to have no awareness of how their behavior is impacting on others.
- **They are usually oblivious to other's feelings.** Like I mentioned in the previous point, emotionally unintelligent people have no idea how their behavior affects others, because they are oblivious to other's feelings. So they say or do insensitive things, and accuse people of being 'too sensitive' when they are confronted about their bad behavior.
- **They lack empathy.** They can't seem to connect with anyone's struggles or feelings.
- **They have poor coping skills.** They have an inability to cope with emotionally charged situations, so they often walk away from such situations to avoid dealing with the emotional fallout.
- **They focus mostly on what is wrong.** They show a lack of positivity and believe everyone needs to improve. So they give out a lot of criticisms and negative feedbacks, and blame others for their own problems.

From the above characteristics highlighted, let's **analyze Dave's behavior in the sample scenario earlier given.**

- He has no emotional self-control and showed no efforts to manage his emotions.
- He could not take criticisms, and began acting in a defensive and aggressive manner
- He refused to cooperate and listen even when his wife was opening up about an issue that bothered her
- He found it difficult to apologize for hurting his wife and was rather stuck on defending his belief that the current incident was a one-time thing and not a pattern of abusive behavior

- He was set on proving that Sandra was the one lying and that he was correct.
- He didn't care how his bad habits affected his wife and was unwilling to hear about it
- He made an insensitive comment about her weight just to shut her up and hurt her.
- He walked out of the house, to avoid the emotional fallout he had caused without a word of apology.

You consider him a terrible person to live with too right? Emotionally unintelligent are difficult people to live with, to work with and to hang with. They say mean insensitive things and do not care if it's hurtful or not. Sometimes, they don't understand that those words are hurtful because they lack empathy.

What are the practical ways to boost my emotional intelligence (EQ)?

Like I have mentioned earlier, emotional intelligence is key to a successful marriage in your life, and it can be learned and developed.

Here are strategies for developing your emotional intelligence:

Do an honest self-evaluation. Have the courage to look at yourself honestly. Evaluate your past actions and thoughts and identify your weaknesses. Are you willing to accept that you are not perfect and that you could work on some areas to make yourself a better person? Self-evaluation is the first step in improving your EQ (emotional quotient).

Observe how you react to people. Are you prone to rush into judgments before you know all of the facts? Do you stereotype? Look deeply and honestly at how you interact with other people.

Examine how you react to stressful situations. Do you become upset every time something doesn't happen the way you want? Do you blame others or become angry at them, even when it is not their fault? Do you lash out at everything and everyone around you when you are upset? Your ability to stay calm and in control in difficult situations needs to be cultivated. Keep your emotions under control when things go wrong. Do not react immediately to tense situations in an angry or confrontational manner, instead slow down your reaction and think carefully before responding.

Learn to be empathetic. Empathy is the ability to identify with and understand the wants, needs, and viewpoints of people around you. Try putting yourself in their shoes, and be more open and accepting of people's perspectives and needs.

Take responsibility for your actions. Whenever you hurt someone's feelings, apologize directly. Do not ignore what you did or avoid the person. People are usually more willing to forgive and forget if you make an honest attempt to make things right. Do not also blame others for your mistakes, own it! Apologize and learn from the experience

Before you take any action, ask yourself 'how will my actions affect others?' Be aware of how your actions affect others by putting yourself in their shoes. Would you want that experience if you were to be in their place? If you must take that action, how can you help others deal with the effects?

Don't just make personal decisions when it comes to your marriage, without explaining them to your spouse first. This is particularly important when the decision will cause great change to happen or is already happening. Don't start making a decision and expect your spouse to run with it, without explaining the reason behind the decision. Your spouse needs to hear what the options were, why and how a particular option was chosen and how it will affect everyone.

Tackle difficult conversations with gentleness and openness. First, ask the other person to share their point of view. Resist speaking up while they talk, listen attentively to understand them, do not go on the defensive right away. Now help the other person understand your point of view, by using clear communication and keeping your tone calm. Then reach a compromise based on what you have learned about each other's views.

Learn to appreciate people's uniqueness and give compliments easily. Emotionally intelligent people know the right things to say to make others happy. They are positive people. Give others a chance to shine, put the focus on them, they would love you better and feel respected.

7
PRACTICE EXERCISE

Find a comfortable spot in your house, make sure you are free from all distractions like technology and people.

Practice mindfulness meditation with a focus on appreciating the people and things in your life that makes it possible for you to live a relatively comfortable and good life. Mediation is a very effective tool for increasing your overall self-awareness, thankfulness and induce relaxation. While meditating, give conscious appreciation and thanks to things, people or phenomena in your life that go unnoticed. By being appreciative of what you often consider insignificant or redundant in your day-to-day life you can start increasing the level of your emotional intelligence.

AFTERWORD

Emotional intelligence is key to bonding better with your spouse and achieving a beautiful and long-lasting marriage. It is an awareness of your actions and feelings – and how they affect those around you. It also means that you value others, listen to their wants and needs, and are able to empathize or identify with them on many different levels.

The advantages are numerous, and it will help you get through life on a smooth sail.

TOPIC 2:

The foundations of a dialogue

–A HONEST COMMUNICATION
What is a dialogue? And why is it important for my marriage?

When we talk about a dialogue, we are referring to a conversation held between two or more people in which thoughts and ideas are exchanged. Constant and consistent dialogues are important for your marriage, they are in fact necessary for its sustenance. You both need to talk to each other, laugh with each other and relax together. Without these, the marriage is dying and on a fast track to divorce. Giving each other the silent treatment for long stretches at a time shows the flaw in the marriage and communicates the anger and unease of both partners.

And we all can tell that a Silent treatment is a sign that something is wrong and needs to be fixed, urgently.

What should be the foundation of dialogues in marriage?

As much as constant dialogues are important in a marriage, you have to note that every of these dialogues must be based on the foundation of **'openness and honesty'**. If not, why even bother? Without this laid-down foundation of openness and honesty, your dialogues would be superficial and ineffective. So for the consistent growth of your marriage and for a stronger emotional & physical bond, you need your dialogues to be impactful, and that is why it has to be really open and authentic.

Now you might be wondering '**what is an open and honest dialogue?**'

It is much easier to explain it by describing what it entails. As a couple, when you and your spouse practice open and honest communication, both of you are able to talk freely and openly about everything and anything.

When you talk, you both keep it respectful and avoid presenting issues in an accusatory manner or including hurtful and insensitive insults. You both listen attentively and try to understand what the other partner is saying.

You both feel safe sharing your most private thoughts with each other. You are both comfortable voicing your worries and feelings to each other without fear of judgment or criticism.

You both don't hesitate or hold back on expressing your gratitude and admiration for each other. And at the end of such talks, both of you should feel satisfied that your concerns and thoughts have been heard, understood and acknowledged.

Now take a moment to bask in all the positive feelings that an open and honest dialogue evokes. Can you feel that warmth, safety, peace, comfort, positivity, freedom, respect, beautiful resolution, and a large serving of happiness? Don't you want to get all of that? I'm sure you do. Do you also notice how the word 'each other' repeats several times in the description? That is because you both are a team, always remember that. You are the strongest bond there is. And you both are building your marital connection and communication for each other, so that you both can feel safe and happy in your bond.

Now I understand that it can be especially hard to have an open and honest dialogue when trying to discuss difficult issues. This is why a lot of couples enroll for marriage counseling sessions. These therapy sessions strive to improve the communication between couples by creating the right ambiance for both parties to completely open up and discuss pressing issues with all honesty.

It is truly understandable that a lot of couples experience poor communication in their marriage. This is because a marriage consists of two people coming from varying backgrounds and having different upbringings and experiences, meaning that both of them would have different ways of communicating their thoughts, wants and needs. This can certainly lead to difficulties in communication. This poor communication can be frustrating for both parties.

9

POOR COMMUNICATION? WHAT DOES IT MEAN?

Poor communication is defined as **the inability of the speaker to convey his/her thoughts and ideas** in such a manner that 'what is heard and understood' by the listener is exactly 'what was meant' by the speaker. **This means that poor communication occurs when there is a disparity** (another word for it is 'mismatch') **between what is being said and what is being heard and understood by the listener.** An example of such poor communication is when a husband asks "What's for dinner?" and his wife understands it as meaning "So you haven't cooked dinner? What have you been doing all day?!", even though what the husband meant by his words is 'what are we eating tonight?'

People with poor communication skills experience difficulties expressing their thoughts in such a way that they can be understood by others. As you may infer, poor communication causes frustration in both the speaker and listener.

What are the Effects of poor communication skills?

Poor communication skills can perpetuate destructive patterns in couples, and can be extremely damaging to the marriage. Below are some effects of poor communication between couples:

- **Poor communication skills evoke feelings of neglect,**

mistrust, animosity, and frustration. When a partner is feeling constantly neglected, invalidated or misunderstood by his/her spouse, the person becomes discouraged with the marriage. This creates insecurities in the person that might lead him/her to seek someone outside of the marriage to fill this void created by the marriage. This basically means a neglected partner or a misunderstood spouse might choose to seek outside validation and fulfillment from a third party to satisfy what he/she feels the marriage is lacking.

- Secondly, **poor communication skills always leads to little or no communication in marriage.** Because really when there is a constant mismatch between what is heard and what is said, why even bother talking right? The constant frustration leads to bad blood and the silent treatments become a frequent occurrence. Now that we have established that poor communication skills cause a total lack of communication, let's see the effects of this lack on the marriage:

- **When there is a lack of communication in marriage, the relationship becomes stagnant.** Marriage consists of two dynamic individuals. Individuals that are always changing and growing as the years go by. This fact makes it very necessary that you never stop learning about each other. Poor communication in marriage is disastrous for the relationship because eventually both parties will become strangers to each other, and become nothing more than roommates. And so as a couple, you both need to learn to evolve together. By doing so, you create a trusting and loving relationship where you both fully understand the other person's wants and needs.

- **Lack of communication causes an emotional distance between your spouse and you.** Talking is how you connect. It is how you express your joy, love, sorrow, gratitude, anger, admiration, wants, needs. It is how your partner learns to understand you. When there is a lack of communication in marriage, love begins to fade. Constant

communication is what keeps both of you interested in one another.
- **When there is poor communication in marriage, both parties will find it difficult to work through their emotions and solve their conflicts.** Poor communication means there is little or no room for compromise. And if you as a person refuse to compromise over certain issues in your marriage, you are basically invalidating your partner's feelings, needs and wants. And it becomes impossible to resolve conflicts.
- **When couples are not open and honest with one another, it becomes common for both of them to start making assumptions about the other.** Imagine this, you come home late several times in a week, without letting your partner know when you would be back or what you were doing, it is quite easy for your spouse to assume you are cheating on him/her. Imagine you are exhausted one evening, and turn down sex without letting your partner know why, your partner may assume you are bored of them and feel neglected. If you refuse to communicate and bottle up personal problems, your spouse may assume that they are the source of your anxiety. Assumptions are never right and are always damaging, so speak up and begin communicating openly and honestly with your partner.

How do you identify poor communication in your marriage?

Now you might be wondering if the communication in your marriage might be described as poor. An easy way to figure this out is by deep reflection, ask yourself these questions:

How often have you walked away from a conversation with your partner with the overwhelming feeling of anger, disappointment or frustration from being misunderstood?

How often have you said things to your spouse that you regretted and wish you could unsay?

How often have you mentioned or done things that hurt your partner unnecessarily?

How often, in the heat of an argument, have you forgotten to be kind, loving, understanding and patient, with your spouse?

How often do you guys neglect to or refuse to ask each other about how your days went?

How often do you give each other the silent treatment?

If you answered 'very often', 'too frequently' or 'all the time', then you have figured out the problem—poor communication skills. Don't panic now. Many people don't know how to communicate effectively, many are just not comfortable voicing out their needs or just don't know how to. The Good news is **Open and Honest Communication skills can be learnt** and with constant practice you would be creating a healthy and happy marriage.

Now let take a breather here and explore this story:

"Sam, are you cheating on me?"

The suddenness and unexpectedness of that question makes him halt his movements, his expression one of shock and confusion. They had just now been laughing at a joke he just shared, how did the conversation abruptly turn this way? He drops the piece of laundry he had been folding and turns to her "Why would you think that?"

"Answer me" Vanessa crosses her arms protectively across her chest, steeling herself for the answer.

"No", he answers, hurt by her assumptions. The hurt slowly gave way to anger.

"Then how are you spending all your earnings? If there isn't another woman in the mix, we should both be able to account for how you spend your money, and our money". They were pretty broke at the moment. Sam had withdrawn most of the cash in their joint account, on grounds of a pretty neat investment opportunity they had to get into. Two weeks later, he had told her he had given all of the cash in his own savings account as a loan to their family friend, Abdul. She had had to immediately adjust the family expenses to fit her little savings and both their salaries. A year later, and all of her savings is gone. they were currently sustaining their household of 4 on their monthly salaries —although, somehow, every of his salary earnings finished rapidly on purchases he usually couldn't account for. She was getting to the bottom of this today. And if he was cheating on her, that b*tch whoever she was better go into hiding.

Sam rubs his forehead with his thumb and index finger in frustration, not this same topic again. "I thought we've been over this"

"No, we haven't!" She snaps. Their last conversation about how their finances were being managed and spent had consisted of him over-enthusiastically explaining that their investments were about to return massive yields in a few weeks. She had believed him, but noticed how he avoided talking about the supposed loan he had given their family friend a year ago. Then earlier that morning, she finds out that they were all lies —He didn't lend Abdul any money. If he was lying about that, then he was definitely lying about the supposed investments. She had spent all morning searching for files and documents related to the supposed investments and found nothing, she even checked his email.

"But I told you already..."

She cuts him off "no, you gave a bunch of excuses that don't add up. I'm not stupid Sam. I can tell when a person is hiding stuffs from me. I can tell when you are lying"

Of a truth, Sam wasn't cheating on his wife. He loved her too dearly, and the thought of being with any other person asides her repulsed him.

"Good! Then you can tell that I'm not lying when I say I'm not cheating on you. I never will!"

Vanessa watches her husband's expression searching for the tell-tale signs that he was lying. She could see he was being honest and gave a tired sigh. "Then what are you hiding from me? What aren't you telling me?"

"Nothing. I'm always transparent with you"

"No you are not, you are not transparent with our Finances Sam! You lied about lending Abdul money. You are lying about the investments." She takes in a deep breath to steady her emotions before asking in a whisper "There is no investment, right?"

Sam gives a defeated sigh before sitting on the bed. He pats the spot beside him, motioning for her to join him. He knew he couldn't lie anymore, not when she was onto him and was watching to see if he was lying. The truth is he had a gambling problem. He nervously fidgets with his wedding ring as he watches her lift herself from her seated position on the plush bedroom rug, and join him on the bed.

He mentally steels himself as he utters the truth he had been hiding all along "I have a gambling problem"

Now pause....

This couple are about to have an open and honest conversation about a difficult issue. Many of us have had to face difficult situations like this —facing super charged situations that span through every difficult topic in the book. I'm not going to sugarcoat this for you, having an open and honest communication on difficult issues is hard in any relationship. They are usually thoughts of "what will she/he think of me?", "Would I be exposing myself to unnecessary vulnerability?" "Maybe I should keep this to myself", "would speaking out permanently ruin things between us?". But you need to confront these potential risks and vulnerabilities. Because by doing so, you are positioning yourself and your partner to reach a higher level of understanding, respect, acceptance, love and trust for each other. So you see why It is necessary to have these dialogues? Because you have to sustain and grow your relationship.

Looking at the above scenario, we see that because Sam was bottling up his gambling problem and being dishonest with their financial record, Vanessa was led to the assumption that he was cheating on her. This is what poor communication does, it leads to unhealthy assumptions, feelings of neglect, mistrust and frustration. Now at this point, if Sam and Vanessa refuse to address this major issue in all honesty or they do it poorly, then they will be headed for a nasty future.

So to avert this nasty future situation, they need to practice open and honest communication. Now in the following subtopics, I will be explaining the importance of honest dialogues in your marriage, and giving practical tips on how to navigate difficult topics in such a way as to reach a reasonable solution. Are you ready? Let's dive in!

Why are constant, honest and open dialogues important?

- **Because poor or little communication implies that you have no Interest in your partner's life.** It is important to constantly and openly communicate with your partner so that you know what is happening in their life and what issues they may be dealing with. constant communication shows that you are interested in them and their life, and that you are willing to understand and give them the necessary emotional and physical support they desire. If you do not know what issues your partner is dealing with or what might be going on in his/her life, you may not be able to understand or empathize with them. This would slowly and surely lead to a strained relationship, because your partner would infer that you just don't care or have an Interest in their life.

- **It builds a better and stronger emotional connection between the two of you.** When you communicate, you express your feelings, thoughts and emotions towards your spouse. I want you to Understand that 'showing' your love and affection for your spouse, with your actions, is just as important as 'expressing it in words'. Always remember that being vocal and expressive about your thoughts, intentions and love is a beautiful and heartfelt way of showing your love towards your spouse, and I assure you that it would lead to a better emotional connection between you two.
- **It gives greater marital satisfaction.** The moment you begin to have constant effective communication with your spouse, you are more likely to experience a happy and peaceful relationship. A better communication means you discuss everything with each other, lesser fights or quarrels and resolved issues.
- **It prevents conflict from becoming toxic.** Conflicts are inevitable, but how you respond and diffuse the situation all boils down to your communication skills. When you refuse to communicate your hurt and frustration to your spouse, and you instead hold on to the negative feelings. You let these negative feelings simmer until they become toxic. Then, this toxicity boils over and you blow up at your spouse in such a way that you hurt them deeply and quite possibly ruin the relationship. But that doesn't have to happen if you would just communicate your feelings

openly and honestly from the very beginning. Make sure to communicate before things get ugly.
- It is how you and your spouse stay on the same page.

What are the practical ways to improve my communication and make dialogues more open and honest?

1. **Be honest.** This is the most important and fundamental rule. If what you are saying isn't true, then nothing real is being shared and your communication is superficial. And like I mentioned earlier, why even bother if you are going to lie? When you avoid the truth out of fear of how it may be received, you only build bigger walls in your relationship. Whenever you speak the truth from a place of love, you are reinforcing the strength of your marital connection. It doesn't matter the response, You have to be honest.
2. **Be patient.** It is very important that you are patient with your partner as they work to find the right words to express themselves. Have you ever been in situations where you struggled to find the perfect words to express yourself? We all have. So be empathetic, put yourself in his/her shoes, and exercise patience. Also, do not plan your responses before your spouse has finished sharing his/her perspectives. Be patient, listen to what he/she has to say, with openness
3. **Be Specific with your words.** Whenever you are arguing about something and you want to make a point, make sure you are specific about it. Do not beat around the bush or talk about random insignificant things. Do not generalize by making statements like "You always say/do this". Statements like this may not serve the purpose you employed it for, instead, you may end up hurting your spouse.
4. **Do not play the Blame Games.** It just wouldn't solve anything and lead to more tension, hurt and anger. Even if you are mad at your spouse for doing something wrong, it

is better to put across your point politely rather than hitting your partner with all the blames.
5. **Do not Be Defensive.** Whenever your partner needs to bring out some complaints or issues against you, it is important that you listen to them intently without being defensive about it. I know it is hard to not be defensive, nobody likes being shown their flaws. But you need to know those flaws, make adjustments and strive to overcome them, so that you can become a better person for your spouse. So instead of getting defensive about the issue, make sure to listen and take effective measures to solve the problem.
6. **Make sure to have regular conversations.** No brainer, yeah? You definitely need regular and constant convos to improve your communication. So no matter how busy you schedule gets and no matter how much work you have to do, always make sure to take out some time in the day to have some meaningful conversation with your spouse. **If you are at a lose of what to talk about, get goofy and silly and share some laughs with each other.** Remember regular communication keeps the love flowing in your relationship.
7. **Stop the nagging and taunting.** Nobody likes getting picked on or nagged, or do you? Stop reminding your partner about their past mistakes in a bid to make them feel guilty and shut them up whenever you wish to make a point. It's cruel. Your spouse wants to feel loved and wanted, everyone does. So every time you taunt your partner, it causes deep hurt and true pain. And this affects your relationship.
8. Also, important to note: whenever you have an argument never drag in family members or friends into it. Remember, you are a tight-knit team, settle your issues amicably between each-other.

10

COMMUNICATION BUILDING EXERCISE

This exercise is for both you and your partner. Pick a date and time you are both comfortable with. Choose a part of the house that you both feel comfortable and relaxed in. Take away all the distractions like phones, laptops, Ipads. If you have little kids, have them stay with a trusted person for the time or wait till they are asleep. Now get comfy, snuggle up with warm blankets, your favorite drink and snacks, a notepad and a pen.

Now let's begin.

In both notepads, you both should strive to keep your answers honest and do not hold back. At the end of the exercise, you both will show each other your answers.

Exercise 1:

Write the ways your spouse can get your attention before they begin communicating with you about anything.

–The reason for this is that many times we don't get our spouse's full attention when speaking to them and so whatever we are trying to communicate with our spouse does not fully register.

Your partner could have a multitasking mind that is at a million places at once, so he/she may require that you say their name and make sure they respond before you start telling them anything.

Exercise 2:

Write down the things your spouse could do to alert you, in a

kind and respectful manner, that you might need a moment to calm down during an argument?

Also, What are those things you could do to calm yourself down whenever you start to feel defensive or having a heated argument with your spouse?

–This is because oftentimes when you are in the thick of an argument, frustration and anger takes over and it becomes harder to remember to stay calm and keep your words kind and respectful.

Exercise 3:

Write down the maximum amount of time you would need for breaks, for those times you desperately want to take a break from a heated argument.

–This is because our brains go into a fight or flight mode whenever we are in the middle of an argument, The feeling of frustration, anger and defensiveness, makes it harder to have respectful and meaningful communication. This is why a short break is needed to help you stay grounded and calm your mind. It should be 'a short break', don't let the break drag on for too long, and make sure to find a way to resolve the conflict

At the end of these exercises, exchange notepads. Take your time to study your partner's answers, ask questions to clarify their thoughts, discuss their needs and agree with your spouse on a set time duration for the last exercise.

A recap:

The foundation of every dialogue in marriage should be based on honest communication. Both parties should always seek to understand the other's point of view. Do not assume what the other person is saying, make sure to ask instead, let the person clarify. Because oftentimes, assumptions lead to more misunderstandings. Endeavor to always keep communication kind, patient and respectful.

The above information is integral to a loving, happy and healthy marriage. Put in the effort to be open and honest with your spouse, because doing this will increase your relationship satisfaction and bring you two closer together.

TOPIC 3:

Appreciations and Gratitude

-Scarcity and Abundance

In any marriage, there are two attitudes —an attitude of contempt and an attitude of appreciation. Yours should always strive to cultivate an attitude of appreciation; just as most happy marriages do. Appreciation is at the core of every healthy relationship. We all want to be appreciated for who we are, what we do, and what we achieve. We all want to know that we are important in other people's lives. We all want to be noticed and valued, it's demoralizing when you are not recognized for your value and skills. The aim of this topic is to teach you why it is important to appreciate your spouse always, and how to show your gratitude for their efforts, in both times of abundance and of scarcity.

12

WHAT IS APPRECIATION? WHAT IS GRATITUDE?

*B*oth are similar in a sense
Gratitude is synonymous to thankfulness, gratefulness, and appreciation. It is from the Latin word 'gratis' meaning 'pleasing, thankful'. Gratitude is the feeling of appreciation felt and shown by the recipient of a kindness (gifts, help, favors, or other types of generosity,) towards the giver of such generosity.

Appreciation is the recognition of the good qualities of someone or something. When you appreciate someone, you are recognizing the person as valuable because of their personality, ability and uniqueness. By showing gratitude and appreciation to your spouse, you are regarding him/her as a valuable gift.

The reasons Appreciation is important for your marriage

As I earlier mentioned, appreciation is at the core of every healthy and lasting relationship. The following are reasons you should imbibe the spirit of constant appreciation:

1. **It makes yourself and your spouse happy:** Showing gratitude to your spouse would definitely make him/her happy. By showing them that they are important in your life and are valued, you will make them feel better about

themselves. You would also feel happy because you have done something to make your spouse smile and feel good.
2. **It Builds Trust:** Gratitude makes us more trusting, nicer, more loving. Appreciation makes the recipient more committed to the giver and makes him/her more likely to stay in the relationship.
3. **It Motivates your partner to do more:** Appreciation is an effective way of motivating anyone. When you praise or appreciate your spouse, it shows that you have recognized their efforts and are grateful. This will encourage them to go the extra mile next time because they are certain they will get even bigger praises and a grander gesture of gratitude from you.
4. **It shows respect for your partner.** When you appreciate someone, you show that you respect their efforts and what they bring to the table.
5. **It deepens your marital connection:** When you adopt a mentality of appreciation rather than contempt (that is, you choose to show gratitude for the good things rather than focus on the bad habits), you will begin to notice just how interesting your spouse is as a person. **Both of you will begin to engage at a much higher and intimate level.** It will amplify the feelings of love in your union and enhance both your impressions about each other.
6. **It gives your partner a sense of relevance:** Feeling appreciated adds a sense of relevancy to your life. You feel important through your connections to other people.
7. **It grows a positive sense of self-worth:** appreciation nourishes a positive sense of self-worth. This is the reason a lot of people's self-esteem is often significantly lower when they feel unappreciated.
8. Gratitude amplifies love, and allows forgiveness: people who constantly give thanks are more likely to experience positive emotions and satisfying interactions. When a couple is committed to seeing and appreciating each other's value and presence, their perspectives on life and their marriage changes and broadens. They feel loved, and

reciprocate the love in return. And because of love, it is easier to forgive errors and mistakes.

9. **Gratitude enhances a better sex life:** When a couple truly feels mutual thankfulness, it deepens their emotional bonds, which inevitably fosters a more intense physical connection (Emphasis on the intense). I don't know about you but I know sex is better enjoyed when it's with someone that values you and you aren't frustrated with.
10. **You both feel comfortable and safe being vulnerable with each other:** When you appreciate one another authentically, it becomes much easier to be open with each other. It is easier to confide with your spouse about your struggles and fears, and be vulnerable. Affirmation creates a safer space to be open and vulnerable with your spouse, and fosters a more tender connection.
11. **Gratitude helps you remember the reasons you fell in love with your spouse in the first place.** When you appreciate precious times spent together and each other's beloved qualities, it sparks memories of your earlier times together. It reignites your passions and intensity, and sustains it even during harder seasons.

Let's take a look at Liam's life:

Liam had been having a rough time at work the past couple of months. He got a query and a salary deduction for failing to meet up with his deadlines for the previous year. He had been struggling to meet up with his new deadlines and goals, but it feels like his skills and knowledge were not enough to get the work done at the time stipulated. This depressing thought has caused him to be perpetually sad, angry and walking around with a defeated demeanor. He had sleepless nights and tired mornings. He had lost appetite for meals and struggled to concentrate on anything aside from work. His wife, Betty, could see how work was affecting his self-esteem and mental health. It caused her great sadness watching her husband suffer this way. So one weekend, she drags him out of the house for a walk around their neighborhood. She was certain the fresh air and nice scenery would do him some good. She was right, the walk seemed to calm him down, he laughed easily at all her jokes and the tenseness in his muscles seemed to ease away. She decided right then and there that she was gonna make the evening strolls a new weekend ritual because that seemed to cheer her husband up. The following Monday, at 12 noon, Liam receives a package of expensive chocolates, a nicely patterned silver cuff-links and his favorite wine with a hand-written note that says *'I love you so much baby. You are smart, talented and hardworking. Your creativity and smartness is dazzling and amazing. I'm sure you are gonna be recognized for it someday soon. I am forever grateful that I have you as my lover, and the kids are blessed to have you as their father. Love, Betty.'*

The sweetness of the gesture made Liam feel light with relief, like a heavy weight was off his chest and shoulders. a warm feeling spread across his chest and a deep-seated feeling of security and assurance bloomed. And for the first time in a long while, he felt like he could achieve anything.

Isn't this sweet? Do you see how an appreciative note and loving gesture turned Liam's mood around?

Betty could have chosen to be angry at Liam's defeated and sad demeanor, she could have nagged him to 'man up', she could have felt resentment at his 'difficult behavior', but she didn't. Because all these negative emotions and reactions would not help matters, instead they would cause a deep rift in the marriage and break up their beautiful union.

She instead chose the path of love and appreciation, she reminded him that she was grateful she had him, and made him feel special and loved.

13

WHAT LACK OF APPRECIATION CAUSES

The feeling of unappreciation means that you feel that your value or contribution isn't appreciated enough in a situation. If your partner feels constantly unappreciated, it could lead to several negative consequences, such as:

- **It leads to constant resentment:** When you feel that you do the majority of the hard work and heavy lifting in the relationship, without getting acknowledged and appreciated for it, it fuels the feeling of resentment in you.
- **It affects one's self-esteem negatively:** When a person feels that his/her spouse takes him or her for granted and couldn't care less if he/she was around, it leaves a harmful effect on the person's self-esteem. The persistent feeling that one doesn't add much value or contributions to his/her spouse's life could do some major damage to that person's self-esteem. So whenever you are vocal about your gratitude, your spouse hears, feels and knows that they are valued.
- **It leads to isolation and emotional withdrawal:** A constantly unappreciated person would begin to isolate his or herself and emotionally withdraw from the marriage, because why bother trying if your efforts would go unnoticed?

- **It leads to depression:** the constant feeling of being unappreciated and constantly ignored by your lover could lead many into depression.
- **It might probably lead to mental illness in the person that feels constantly unappreciated:** if your spouse seems to ignore what you do for them, it can cause feelings of devastation and frustration. You might begin to wonder if all the things you do for your spouse are really worth the effort, and might stop trying.

How can you tell if your spouse feels unappreciated?

The signs are these:

- Your spouse has begun to emotionally distance his/herself from the marriage and has become quieter than usual
- Your spouse doesn't make any effort to be romantic anymore
- Your spouse has stopped being enthusiastic about special occasions and anniversaries
- Your spouse no longer asks for your opinion about personal issues.
- Your spouse has become more aggressive lately and is lashing out at everyone with frustration and anger
- Your spouse seems 'always eager' to get into arguments over little things
- Your spouse is making decisions and plans without even consulting you

14

WHAT ARE WORDS OF AFFIRMATION AND AFFECTION?

Words of affirmation are any spoken or written words that confirm, uplift, support, and empathize with another person in a positive manner. Words of affirmation is one of the five love languages. Appreciation is at the heart of having words of affirmation as a love language. Words of affirmation means you are constantly appreciating your partner's looks, abilities, personality and values. It recognizes quality over quantity and substance over appearance.

Did you note the words of affirmation in Betty's note to Liam. Here it is again: *'I love you so much baby. You are smart, talented and hardworking. Your creativity and smartness is dazzling and amazing. I'm sure you are gonna be recognized for it someday soon. I am forever grateful that I have you as my lover, and the kids are blessed to have you as their father. Love, Betty.'*

She affirmed her love for him. She affirmed his importance in her life and that of their kids. She made him feel wanted, needed and treasured. And she affirmed all his winning qualities (qualities he was beginning to doubt): '...*You are smart, talented and hardworking. Your creativity and smartness is dazzling and amazing...*'

What do we mean by Scarcity and Abundance?

Scarcity refers to a state of lack, while Abundance refers to a state of surplus.

When we use the words 'scarcity' and 'abundance' in this topic, we mean it in the financial sense of the word. So in this context, **scarcity would mean the times when you are broke or financially struggling, and abundance would mean the times when you are financially comfortable or have a huge account balance** (yup, rich!)

So we should be grateful and appreciative even when we are broke?

Yes! always be grateful and appreciative, EVEN WHEN YOUR SPOUSE IS BROKE AND FINANCIALLY STRUGGLING!

How would you feel if you were only shown to be loved, valued and appreciated only when you are rich? Like your self-worth was only measured by how much money you have? Bad right? Exactly! Appreciate your spouse, for the person he or she is. Show gratitude for the things they do, for the good feelings they bring to you, for their company, for them. Money should not be a deciding factor of when to show appreciation and gratitude.

How do you show appreciation and gratitude to your spouse?

- **Say Thank you! Be vocal about it, and say it more often:** make it an intentional habit, make it a fundamental part of you. Because saying 'thank you' is the simplest and most obvious way to show your gratitude to your spouse. Always make sure to say it regularly. Those two simple words go a long way. It can be easy to neglect to say thank you for those everyday tasks that may seem mundane, but don't neglect to say it. Appreciate them if they iron your clothes or cook your meal, take out the trash, or wash your car. By constantly saying 'thank you', you will see that your frequent appreciation will transform your spouse's view of those boring tasks, and make them more excited to do it, especially if he or she has been feeling frustration at

doing it before. Thanking them for little things makes a big difference.
- **Behave in a grateful manner:** Saying "thank you" is not quite enough, in fact it is just the first step. you shouldn't just stop at the verbal appreciations, show it too! in your thoughts and actions. You have to behave in a grateful way toward your spouse. Don't take him or her for granted and take care to make sure that you are not undermining or undoing their efforts in any way.
- **Splurge on a thoughtful 'just because' gift:** Because you are constantly grateful to have your spouse, surprise him or her once in a while with a gratitude gift. Buy something you noticed your spouse would like to have but is not willing to buy for himself or herself, then attach a little note of thanks before you give it. For example, your wife has been admiring a watch or a dress for a while now, but she hasn't bought it for herself. You could use it as a perfect opportunity to buy her the object of her desire. Your spouse will definitely appreciate the thoughtfulness and be so happy.
- **Take your spouse on a romantic date or trip.** Take your spouse on romantic dates and trips that will make romance novels and movies yell 'Goals!!!'. Make that time all about your spouse. Flirt with them, seduce them, shower them with compliments and give your full and undivided attention. Romantic dates are a great way to say thank you to your husband or wife for everything they do and mean to you. And to remind them you are most definitely still madly in love, and are happy in the love.
- **Write a sweet and thoughtful note, letter or card.** Hide it where your spouse can easily find it. It is beautifully fascinating how a little note like that can brighten someone's day. So grab a sticky note, scribble a sweet thank you message and stick it to your bathroom mirror or the fridge. I assure you that this gesture can make all of your lover's daily efforts feel more worthwhile.
- **Give your spouse a break, some rest, some alone time.**

Especially when your spouse is feeling overworked or overwhelmed, make sure to give them a few hours of quiet time or a break from their regular tasks. Let him or her relax, let them feel pampered by you. The break could mean you taking over their chores for the day, and giving them some alone time to catch up on movies, books, sleep or go out.

- **Let other people know, as often as possible, how grateful you are for your spouse.** This public show of gratitude will please your partner way more than you can imagine. Be vocal about your gratitude among extended family, and friends. let it be known that you are thankful for everything your spouse does for you and your family.
- **Seduce him or her with a special meal.** Good food does wonders. Set aside a little time to cook or place an order for your lover's favorite meal (if you can't cook). Set the table, light some scented candles, play romantic songs, and dine-in together at home.
- **Compliment him or her often:** He or she looks good? Say it! They did something good? Say it! Be vocal about their fine points "babe, I love your new hairstyle. It looks really beautiful" or "babe, I loved the taste of dinner. You are a brilliant cook!" Compliments go a long way to boost their moods.
- **Remind your spouse why you fell in love with him or her.** Be romantic about it, remind your partner the reasons you fell in love with him or her, and why you are still in love. make sure to maintain eye contact and physical touch as you speak.

15

PRACTICAL APPRECIATION EXERCISES

*A*n appreciation exercise is a practical assignment that helps you to express your appreciation for another person by guiding you through it. Happy couples practice gratitude together, they appreciate each other. Below are practical ways to express gratitude with your spouse. The simplest of these exercises will definitely bring a smile to your spouse's face and yours.

- Every night before you both go to bed; **tell your partner three things you appreciate about him or her that day.**
- **Exchange love letters with each other** like you are teenagers all over again.
- On the weekend, **prepare a meal together.** Spend quality time together preparing the meal (or meals) you both enjoy eating, talk about each other's week, joke, sing and dance together. You could pick any other day of the week to do this, make sure both your schedules are cleared for that day.
- **Start saying 'Thank you' for every task your spouse does, and mean it.** It doesn't matter if you consider the task mundane or easy, verbally appreciate your partner's contributions. Make sure to use your body language when communicating your gratitude. Make eye contact, smile or

touch each other lovingly; it could be by giving a hand squeeze, a hug or a kiss.
- **Make a list of all the things you appreciate about your partner and place it where you both can see it easily.** This written record of gratitude will prove powerful and calming on those days either of you feels frustrated or lonely.
- **Make a list of fun activities to try out together.** try out fun and new experiences together like visiting a museum in town, mountain climbing, going on a cruise to a dream location. make an effort to do at least one thing from the list every month. When you and your spouse spend quality time together in an unfamiliar environment, you would both connect with each other in a whole new way.
- **Cuddle time:** This exercise is as simple and fun as it sounds. The instructions are simple: Cuddle. Cuddle a lot! Practice it at convenient times, it could be at bedtime or first thing in the morning when you both wake up or while watching TV – just make sure to choose whatever time works best for you two. The important thing is that you both are getting some one-on-one time, showing physical affection, and enhancing your intimacy. When we cuddle, our mood improves, you feel a deeper connection, you feel safe and sleep better. I suggest that you cuddle to a music playlist, it will set the mood and keep the atmosphere romantic.
- **Ask your partner the areas they feel unappreciated in the marriage and listen to their response.** Set a timer and listen without interruption. Do not speak at all until the timer goes off. Just sit back, listen to your partner and soak it all in. Although you may not speak during this time, you are free to communicate to your spouse non-verbal encouragement and empathy through your body language, facial expressions, and meaningful looks. When the timer goes off, apologize and say thank you for all the things you took for granted. Then, switch roles and try the exercise again.

- **Exchange roles for the day.** I find that it will enable you both to appreciate each other's contribution to your marriage. So take over your spouse's chores for the day and let your spouse take over yours.
- **Give your spouse a break, some rest, some alone time.** Let your spouse have some alone time, especially if he or she feels overworked. Allow your partner rest in bed and catch up on movies, books or sleep, while you take over his or her chore.

AFTERWORD

Appreciation and Gratitude is fundamentally to every healthy relationship, you and your spouse must work hard to cultivate it.

As Les Parrott, a #1 New York Times bestselling author of several marriage advice books, says, "Gratitude can transform common days into Thanksgivings, turn routine jobs into joy, and change ordinary opportunities into blessings."

So choose gratitude and appreciation always! And watch your marriage blossom and bloom.

TOPIC 4:

Negotiation and Compromise

–The different values

Like I had mentioned earlier in Topic 2 (**The foundations of a dialogue –A HONEST COMMUNICATION**), a marriage consists of two different individuals who are coming from varying backgrounds and have different upbringings and experiences. This means they would have different values. Many of these values are influenced by race, culture, religion, and their family orientation. As Humans that we are, we inevitably run into problems whenever our wants and needs don't match that of our partner's.

Couples should be ready to face many unexpected home and lifestyle clashes if they are not prepared to compromise or negotiate. To resolve these problems and enable your 'happily ever after' dreamy marriage, you and your spouse need to become skilled in the fine art of negotiations and compromise. To have a healthy and happy marriage, both partners have to work super hard at having successful negotiations and reaching healthy compromises. And that healthy compromise and successful negotiations is what will keep your union strong, happy and vibrant despite the different values and habits.

17
WHAT DO I MEAN BY NEGOTIATION?

In a negotiation, each person gets something they want in exchange for giving something their partner wants. The difference between negotiation for couples and other negotiations is that the amount of self-disclosure required in a couple's negotiations is higher and requires lots of openness, vulnerability and emotional risk.

18

WHAT DOES IT MEAN TO COMPROMISE?

A compromise is the settlement of a dispute, through an agreement by both parties to make certain concessions.

An example of compromise is this, suppose Ali and Lolade were planning to go out for dinner, and Ali wants seafood at a Chinese restaurant, while Lolade wants jamaican cuisine. After much deliberation, their compromise is to have both meals delivered to their house, so they can eat at home. In other words, neither was forced to eat something they didn't want to eat, but neither also got to go to the restaurant they wanted to see.

You see, compromise can be the resolution to your conflicts or the demise of your marriage. Let me tell you how:

There are two kinds of compromise: the healthy kind and the unhealthy kind.

The healthy kind is the positive side of compromise. In a healthy compromise, both parties agree to meet in the middle by making concessions that are mutually beneficial to both of them i.e they both gain, not lose. Each partner should be happy or satisfied with the outcome of the concessions.

However, **the unhealthy kind** is the acceptance of standards and conditions that are lower than what is desirable. This is the down side of compromise. We don't like this kind.

How do I differentiate between both types of compromise?

The main difference is 'compromise' vs 'sacrifice'. An unhealthy compromise requires you sacrificing your core values, beliefs, needs and personal boundaries, to maintain. It tips the scale too far in the wrong direction. You begin to lose yourself, you sacrifice who you truly are to become a fake version of you. And you can see how it could break a marriage.

Meanwhile the goal of a healthy compromise is to be mutually beneficial. In a healthy compromise, both of you choose to experience the short-lived discomfort of concession in return for the greater future gain of personal growth for each other, leading to a happier relationship and individual happiness.

What are the no-go areas I mustn't compromise?

Compromise is based on a 'give and take' logic, but there must not be give and take on some fundamentals. Your relationship should not infringe on certain core factors. These are the areas where you should not back down, and compromise would actually be ruining your marriage:

- **Your respect:** Do not compromise on your respect! You should always be treated with respect in your relationship. You should both be given the opportunity to engage in the relationship dynamics on equal footing, because you are both equally valid. Do not accept disrespectful or undermining attitudes/actions from your partner. Do not bend your self-respect to conform to your partner's rudeness. So if your partner speaks in a derogatory manner to you and addresses you in such belittling ways, do not accept it as 'a flaw you can compromise on'.
- **Your core values:** Your core values and beliefs are what you use to map your route through life. What you believe in is part of what defines who you are. Such examples of core values are a 'Family First' mentality (meaning you are a family person and would always place your family's needs as priority), no cheating (meaning you value your commitments and faithfulness), no illegal drug usage, no murder, kindness to everyone, no corrupt practices (meaning you wouldn't steal, embezzle, or engage in fraudulent activities). Now imagine your partner trying to

make you compromise on such core values? You would be losing yourself and what makes you 'you'. So when it comes to fundamental value systems, don't compromise who you are, for your relationship. Your partner should love and respect you. If they want to change you in areas essential to your identity, it may be time to admit that you are a mismatch.

- Your **close friends and family:** I don't know what says red-flag more than a partner that tries to manage your other close relationships. That wants to control how you communicate with them and when, and which one of them to communicate with. It is not acceptable for your partner to stop you from communicating with your close family or friends or to limit it. Although you both need to mutually agree on how you both spend your free times, it should not mean that your close connections be controlled. And you should not compromise on your social and emotional support network (that is, close friends and family). Let the decision of whom you talk to be made by you. Although, always make sure to listen to your partner's unease about your particular friend or family that they don't get along with, there is often truth in their words. Find a way to ease your partner's worry and make him/her feel better secured in the relationship.

- **Your plans for your own Future:** your partner should want you to follow your dreams and support your goals. It is not a supportive relationship, if he/she is trying to cut your wings, encouraging you to dream smaller or asking you to do less. If your future is being undermined, don't give it up for the sake of your relationship. An example is this, Smith dreams of being a grammy award winner. Since he was a teenager, he had been working hard at that goal and presently has 3 albums to his name— one of them had even made the grammy award nomination list for two categories. His wife, Katy, on the hand, doesn't think he should pursue this dream of a grammy award because although he's excellent at what he does, she wants him to

retire and focus more on their family life. And maybe work at a law firm since he has a law school degree. Do not compromise on your dreams! You will go through life unsatisfied and with regrets. To journey through life together, you should both be supportive of each other's dreams and aspirations.
- **Your spirituality:** does it even sound right to say "I'll give up my spiritual beliefs for you"? No! Definitely not! Your spiritual beliefs is part of who you are. Do not compromise on it.

Negotiations Vs Compromise: Which should have the priority?

In my personal opinion, negotiated solutions work much better than compromises on a lot of levels. Compromises, although well-intended, get frustrating and build resentment when they are the constant solution to every disagreement because no party is ever truly getting what they want, they are instead agreeing on a middle ground. Either one person entirely gives up what they want, or both do.

Meanwhile in negotiations, each partner gets something they really want in exchange for giving something their partner really wants. Don't get me wrong, compromises are necessary too. But negotiations should be the first step and compromise the next solution if negotiations seem to be failing. Oftentimes, a successful negotiation leads to a healthy compromise. For example, Carolina wants to be the one to choose their first baby's names, while Arthur wants to install a fancy fish pond filled with lots of koi in their backyard. Carolina doesn't want the pond because she is worried about the safety of their future kids. While Arthur doesn't trust Carolina's taste in names because she has an affinity for ancient names and outdated classics. After much deliberation and a successful negotiation, they agree that each will get what they want in exchange for giving something the other wants.

Now both parties have successfully negotiated their terms. Carolina gets to name their first child, and Arthur gets to have a fancy pond filled with the colorful koi he admires. And they make compromises too on the issue. Carolina has to pick a name that was popular after the 1800s, and Paul has to place a high protective fence around the pond and always keep the gates locked when no adult is in there.

You could talk about negotiation without bringing up compromise but there cannot be any talk about compromise without bringing up negotiation. It can be said that a successful negotiation brings about compromise. What I mean by this is 'negotiation uses effective communication methods to lay down one's terms, conditions and needs, and to prevent misconstruing one's words or intentions,' while compromise involves using this effective communication to find a mutual ground and settle differences for the benefit of all parties involved.

A Recap: negotiation and compromises are good. But be careful with the kind of compromises made so that it doesn't become unhealthy and breed contempt and frustration. Healthy compromises should be the goal, because they benefit both parties and bring the relationship closer. Do not compromise if it means lowering your standards for less than you deserve. Healthy compromise is about creating a fair playing field to accommodate both of you. It is not about conceding to a lower standard.

Why is negotiating and compromise necessary in my marriage?

- **You would be solving your conflicts more effectively and in a manner that benefits both of you:** Good negotiation leads to acceptable solutions that are advantageous to both you and your partner. This, in turn, will strengthen your union.

- **You will be teaching and showing your spouse how to treat you:** in negotiating, you are basically building the terms of your relationship. You are clearly stating things you won't tolerate, things you can abide by and things you may compromise on.
- **It solidifies trust and respect in your relationship:** Everytime you negotiate a deal with your spouse and you follow

through on your words, it builds trust and respect in your partner. Your spouse would know that he or she can believe whatever you say and that you can be counted on. think about someone who has broken their promises to you, can you ever rely on such a person? Can you ever believe the person's words again?

- **There will be less arguments and more fun times:** whenever you have both successfully negotiated a conflicting issue, and both of you are living up to your ends of the bargain, there would be less arguments on that issue because it is out of the way now. And since that issue has been resolved, you can both go on to better things and spend more quality time together.
- **For your marriage to work and grow:** A wise person once said "for any relationship to work there has to be some sort of compromise because everyone has flaws. you have to learn to live with said flaws if you truly love them" and I'm sure that makes sense to you too.

Disclaimer: I have to add this bit here, the above is not advice to stick with someone that has toxic flaws. Do not compromise your identity and boundaries to fit an abusive relationship. Remember 'healthy compromise' is the keyword.

What happens if my spouse and I refuse to bend our values and needs to accommodate each other's needs?

1. You ruin the relationship: When you and your partner are both dead set in your individual ways and refuse to accommodate each other's needs or be more flexible with each other, you ruin the relationship. When you approach your relationship with a rigid attitude, and you are unwilling to be flexible and stretch yourself to accommodate your partner's needs, your relationship will get stuck in a place, with no progress, just stagnancy. Learn the wisdom of compromise, for it is better to bend a little than to break.
2. It leads to feelings of dissatisfaction, animosity and

loneliness: Even if you marry the person of your dreams, to live happily ever after, you need to become skilled in the fine art of compromise. If you can't bend to accommodate your partner's needs, your relationship will quickly degrade into feelings of dissatisfaction, discord, loneliness and frustration.
3. You would have more arguments and conflicts: A clash of wants and needs will definitely lead to conflicts. You should be ready to face many clashes if you are not prepared to compromise or negotiate. Also, more conflicts will continue to arise to join the already existing pile of unresolved issues. Until finally, the gigantic heap becomes too much to bear and you both break up the marriage.

Before we head into the next subsection, I would like you to answer a few questions:

- Do you value the differences between your spouse and you?
- Is it okay if you are not right?
- Are you open to learning something new?
- Can you put your needs aside to meet your spouse's needs?
- Can you negotiate your differences with a spirit of love and respect?
- Are you willing to compromise and negotiate on a regular basis?

If you answered mostly "yes," to the questions above, you have the right mindset for healthy compromises and negotiations. your right attitude will definitely give you the pleasantly warm home you desire, and your spouse and you will have a better understanding of each other.

If you answered mostly "no," well... how do I put this? You definitely need a new mindset. I don't want to say your current mindset is problematic, but it is!

But don't you panic now, there's a way out! You can change,

through constant efforts you will become a better person for yourself and for your spouse.

Now moving on to the next!

What are the emotions and attitudes that can interfere with effective negotiation, before it even begins?

- **Self-deprecating thoughts and thoughts that evoke frustration:** "I'm not worthy, I don't deserve it", "I never get what I want", "My partner doesn't care about what I want"
- **An aggressive thought process, selfishness and rigidness:** "What I want is more important than what my partner wants", "I won't let anyone push me around!", "I have to fight for what I want in life", "If I get what I want I will be obligated in the future to give even when I don't want to be giving."
- **Fears:** several fears interfere with successful negotiations. Fears such as fear of offending your partner or disrupting your relationship if you are assertive, the fear of the hurt that would come from not getting what you asked for. Don't let fears stop you.

What are the practical tips to help guide our negotiations and ensure that it doesn't lead to a fighting match?

Take note that there are no laid-out rules or step-by-step procedures to negotiation in marriage because it has to be real and from the heart (non-scripted). However, you do need to keep some tips in mind to prevent the negotiations turning into a screaming match.

1. **Effective communication:** It is important to note that effective communication is needed to communicate your thoughts accurately to your spouse, in order to avoid being misconstrued or misunderstood. It is general knowledge that unless you are married to a psychic or to a fortune teller, you are going to have to learn to communicate effectively with your spouse. Effective communication makes sure that what you speak and mean is exactly what is heard and understood. So if you skipped Topic 2 on **The**

foundations of a dialogue –A HONEST COMMUNICATION, then you should get back to it as soon as you are done with this Topic. Now back to the subject matter, effective communication can be as easy as not giving room for assumptions and also not assuming that your partner should know things because half the time, they do not. If there is anything you are not sure of, ask away!

2. Pair effective communication with **Listening**: Another important thing to do during negotiations is to listen. Always give your spouse a chance to respond and then listen. Do not interrupt their response and allow them to speak. Pay close attention to what they are saying and do not dismiss their thoughts immediately. Just like when haggling prices in the market, you have to listen to the other person's opinion to reach a common ground and finally get something out of the interaction, which is the goal of negotiating. Otherwise, the other person (in this case, your partner) feels like their voice has not been heard and then they feel condescended to or angry or both and there is little or no progress. A plus side to listening is that sometimes, we have assumed wrongly or/and we find out the real reason for certain actions taken by our partners, reasons we were earlier oblivious to. So in order for any negotiation of the sort to be successful, effective communication has to be coupled with listening.

3. Take a moment to **view the situation from a longer perspective**: Always make sure to take a step back from the situation and ask yourself **if this issue will matter in the long run**. In three year's time, does it matter if you had Chinese or Pizza for dinner? Probably not. In five year's time, does it matter if we used our savings to buy a fancy house or go on a dream vacation? Yup, most definitely. Using time as a lens, puts your problem into perspective. You see the problems that require more energy, and the ones that will be insignificant in the long run.

4. **Keep your tone and words polite and respectful.** Do not

speak with malice. Avoid sarcasm and speak with a steady, non-judgmental tone. tell your partner what you feel in a non-condescending way— do not assume a tone of superiority. By non-condescending, I mean communicating in a way that doesn't make the other person feel like less of a person or stupid.

5. **Place yourself in your spouse's shoes:** I don't mean that literally, I mean you should see things from their own perspective. Take a long moment to consider what the situation looks like from your partner's perspective. For example, you want to go on a romantic boat cruise with your partner for your anniversary. But your spouse doesn't want that, and you don't seem to get why. Putting yourself in their shoes, you see that their near-drowning incident a few years back has made him/her scared of large bodies of water. So now you understand, now you are better equipped to understand why your partner is adamant about the boat trip. Seeing things from another perspective is a good way to expand your emotional intelligence and your capacity for empathy. (Now, you see why Topic 1 is important? *wink wink) So begin to ask, how does the situation impact your spouse? What does it feel like from their position? What kind of sacrifices would your spouse be making if he or she went along with your ideas? You should never judge a person until you have walked a mile in their shoes (again, not literally). Looking at your issues from a different point of view might just put things into perspective.

6. **Manage your emotions wisely:** How you react to a situation is half the battle. Don't let your emotions dictate for you. Leaving yourself to the power of your emotions could be disastrous. Keep your cool, you can't achieve much if tempers are flaring. Whenever things get heated, sit back and take a moment to calm down. You have to learn how to best confront an issue without coming from a place of unwarranted anger, and violent emotions. Being calm and focused on the issue at hand will give you a

better chance of having an effective and healthy discussion.

7. **Timing is important:** Make sure there is enough time to talk things out. Negotiations shouldn't be done in a hurry or rushed. Take your time to communicate and listen to each other's point of view.
8. **Be focused:** keep your focus at the issue. Do not ramble about other meaningless things or unrelated matters. Get rid of other distractions like your phones, tablets, laptops or television. You need a 100% focus and your undivided attention when negotiating.
9. **Approach the discussion with openness.** Be open to hearing your partner's point of view without being judgmental nor making comparisons. Be open to the chance that you might be wrong. Be open to the possibility of changing your stance on the matter. Trust me, openness is one of the key mindset for a successful negotiation in marriage.
10. **Look for common ground.** This is the most important part of negotiations and compromises. Always look for that shiny spot of common ground where you and your partner are both comfortable in. That is of course if you value the relationship [and do not want things to fall apart over any and every inconvenience] and are interested in resolving your issues whatever they might be.

19

PRACTICE ACTIVITY:

Select a private spot in the house and choose a comfortable time for this exercise, make sure that it is a time neither of you would be interrupted.

–Sit "knee to knee". This position allows you to physically turn toward each other, and maintain physical and eye contact.

–Pick a topic you and your partner do not agree on, (it could be what person should do a certain chore, what color to repaint your apartment, or bigger stuffs like where to relocate to)

–Now with a notepad and pen, jot down your answers as they come. Take time to discuss some of these questions and the answers.

The questions:

- How important is my choice on the matter to me? And why is it?
- To get what I want, what will I need to do and what will my partner need to do?
- If we agree to do most of what I want, what is the positive and negative effect on my partner?
- What ways could I make it easier for my partner to say yes to my demands?
- If we do not resolve this disagreement, what would the effects be on my marriage?

- What are the effects on you if you get most of what you demand?
- What are the reasons it may be difficult for your partner to give you most of what you want?
- What are the ways you can increase the benefits and decrease the downside to my partner.

AFTERWORD

As the late Jarad Anthony Higgins, professionally known as Juice World, eloquently puts it in the hit song, *smile*: "*I'd do anything in my power to see you just smile*".
    This eloquently sung profession of love just establishes the beautiful truth that at the end of the day, compromise and negotiation is needed if you are willing to make the necessary changes to see that your partner is happy. And thus, what successful relationships have in common is not the absence of inconvenience but the ability and willingness of its partners to negotiate and reach a mutual concession (compromise) whenever a problem arises.

Did you like this book, or did you find it useful, until now?

Your support really makes a difference! I would be very grateful if you would publish an exhaustive review on Amazon. All reviews are read personally, so that I can get real feedback and make this book (and the whole series) even better.

Thanks again for your support!

TOPIC 5:

Relationship with friends

–Extrovert and Introvert
Sub-topic 1:

*H*ow your relationship with friends morphs, evolves and changes after marriage.

Marriage marks a whole new chapter in your life, and it is most likely your biggest transitional period. A long list of things changes when you get married, for example perhaps your last name, your priorities, your residence and living arrangements, your commitments to each other, and many other changes. Many couples are usually prepared for many of these changes, but the one area of change that only a few of us are ready for is 'friendships changing after marriage'. Many are not even aware that their friendships could change after they tie the knot.

Of course, your friends don't become less important after you get married, but the frequency with which you hang out with them naturally wanes once you are married. Don't panic now, it is a totally healthy thing. This is because as you grow and change, your priorities shift, and your friendships tend to adapt to the new you over time. You would also begin to seek and find new friends that will meet your changing needs. What is important is that you hold on to meaningful friendships and let go of the rests that are too hard to maintain.

Again, it is important that you remember it is perfectly normal for your friendships to change after you get married. It is just how life is and how relationships grow and evolve.

But even if you have limited time to hangout with your friend, or maybe no time at all, there is no reason to give up the friendship entirely. It just would require extra work and both of you adjusting to the new changes.

So, what are the ways your friendships could change after marriage?

1. They would require more effort than previously needed. To keep your friendships alive in this stage of your life, you are going to have to put extra efforts into them. Before marriage, it may have been easier to balance your time with your boyfriend/girlfriend and your friends. But after marriage, your spouse by default takes up more time. so it becomes necessary that you might need to put more effort into clearing your schedule in order to meet up with your friends.
2. They will require more intentional planning and extra attention to maintain. When you are single, you probably see your friends out of sheer convenience, it may be because you live together, you go to school together, or you go to the same workout classes. But once you get married, you begin spending almost every waking and non-working hour with your new family, because your spouse is now the main priority. So maintaining your friendships requires intentional planning that might have not previously been needed. Intention means scheduling time to hangout in advance, calling or texting to communicate your commitments and time limitations to your important friends. It will also require discussing with your partner, how you plan to continue and maintain your significant friendships.
3. Your Friendships will either strengthen or weaken. I'm not

going to sugarcoat this for you, the truth is everyone reacts to change in different ways. While some of your friendships might get stronger after you get married, some others may end. Some of your friends may not adapt to the married you, and may choose to create distance. This distance is usually a sign that they are not ready or able to adjust to your new identity, and needs. If you ever notice that a friend is avoiding you after you get married, it is best to have an honest conversation with him or her. Talk to that friend about their feelings so you can both come to a better understanding of what is going on and the next step for your friendship.

4. There is an exciting possibility for couple friendships: Couple friendships mean being friends with another couple. Couple friendships are exciting and fulfilling in ways that differ from your usual friendships. You now get to have double dinner dates, shared couple vacations and attend special events with another couple, this can create a stronger bond that will last for life. Think of family friends!

5. Your conversations may shift from being majorly in person to being majorly through texts and calls. Because of limited free time, you may just have to communicate majorly through texts with friends. This is especially true if you have kids in the picture. Physically hanging out will require that you get a babysitter to watch the kids before you can go out. And you also would have to check with your friends to make sure your schedules mutually align. So because of all these planning and efforts, friends often neglect the regular in-person dates and instead turn to texting and phone calls more.

21

SUB-TOPIC 2:

How your Friendships could affect your marriage –The extrovert and introvert's compromise

Scott and Malia had just gotten home from a long night of karaoke and drinking with Malia's friends. Scott could tell Malia was upset, she had been shooting him angry glares at intervals from the very moment he had refused to get on the stage to sing along to a romantic song by Ed Sheeran, despite all her friends eager pleadings that he does so. In his defense, although he loved singing and had a great voice, he was an introvert whose social anxiety got really intense at the prospect of singing in front of a crowd. He was fine singing at home, with no one but his wife listening to him. He felt more comfortable with her than with anyone else in the world.

He unbuttons his shirt slowly as he watches Malia angrily take off her short dress and shove it unceremoniously into the closet. Okay, he would bite.

"Baby, what's wrong?" He asks

She turns towards him, the anger evident in her expression, and yells "What the f*ck is wrong with you? Why don't you ever try to get along with my friends? I put so much effort getting along with both of your friends, why wouldn't you do the same for mine?" It was true, Scott had only two close friends —Jones and Adey. Their interests and personalities were vastly different from hers, but she had made sure to always keep in touch with them both and send them thoughtful gifts once in a while. They had both gotten very accustomed to her and were now close friends with her too.

Scott is stunned by her sudden outburst and stares awhile at her, trying to form the right words to accurately communicate his thoughts and intentions. The words don't seem to come, so he continues to stare wordlessly at her.

His continued silence infuriates her further and she walks past him into the bathroom to wash off her makeup and get ready for bed. He lets out a deep sigh, and makes to sit on the bed before making a quick-thinking decision to follow her into the bathroom. He couldn't go to bed knowing she was mad at him.

"Look honey, I can tell I have made you upset. I'm sorry" he begins as soon as he gets into the bathroom.

She stops the angry wiping of her face to listen to him.

He continues "But you know I'm trying my best. You know how much hanging out with unfamiliar people makes me nervous and uncomfortable."

Malia calms down at the realization that she had neglected to see things from his own perspective, she drops the makeup cleansing wipes onto the sink and goes to give him a hug.

Still maintaining the hug, she whispers into his chest "couldn't you try to know them better? I swear they would feel familiar once you get to know them. You would like them"

"I'm trying. That's why I was out with you guys tonight. I skipped my online gaming tonight to be with you." He answers. He lets his hands hold her tightly to his chest, the physical contact calming him down.

Malia felt grateful for his gesture and intentions, as she understood the sacrifice he had made to be out with her tonight. He and his best friends usually played online games together at least thrice in a week, and she knew how much he loved gaming.

"I'm sorry I got upset. It's just that I had been bragging to my friends how good of a singer you are. And it had hurt me when you refused to sing in front of them. I felt like your refusal would make them doubt my earlier brags"

"I understand. But I could never sing in front of Jones and Adey, and I've known them since I was 6"

His honesty brings a smile to her face, they were both going to be alright, she knew it.

From the above story, we see how an introverted partner and an extroverted partner could have clashes and frictions because of differences in their needs. And we can see how loving compassion and effective communication can resolve these clashes.

Who is an extrovert and who is an introvert? What is the difference?

An extrovert is someone who is outgoing, sociable and socially confident. The character traits of an extrovert are:

- They prefer spending their time around other people and dislike being alone.
- They like crowds, parties and other gatherings with lots of new people
- They need quality time with other people to help them recharge and boost their energy
- They are talkative, outgoing, and enjoy being the center of attention.

While an introvert is someone who focuses primarily on their own mind, feelings and affairs. The character traits are:

- They enjoy spending time alone in a space they find comfortable.
- They prefer having quality time with one or two people than spending time with bigger groups of friends.
- They need alone time to recharge and rest after a busy workday or period of activity.
- They get lost in their thoughts quite easily and often need time to process and think things through.

The biggest difference between the two is in how each personality prefers to spend their time. Introverts enjoy spending more time alone and recharging in solitude. They are very aware of their internal thoughts because they spend more time with themselves.

Extroverts are the opposite, they are outspoken, outgoing and absolutely love being around other people. That is what really refuels and gets them happy.

Another difference is that extroverts feel refreshed after connecting with many people and being with a crowd, while introverts may feel drained and exhausted by that same experience.

So yeah, in case you hadn't realized, Malia is the extroverted partner and Scott is an introvert.

Can knowing if your spouse is introverted or extroverted help your relationship?

Yes, it does. The more information you know about your partner's personality, the better it is for your marriage.

Knowing will help you understand your partner better, reduce conflicts, and will greatly improve your quality of life and overall happiness. When you know that your husband or wife is an introvert, you may not be shocked when he/she turns down your offer to go to a loud, crowded bar over the weekend. And you would understand when he or she opts instead for a movie and ice cream night at home with you. Having this knowledge will help you avoid taking the rejection personally since you know it is not about you, but more about what your spouse needs to feel comfortable.

Another scenario is when you know that your husband or wife is extroverted, you would understand why they enjoy dressing up and attending parties. And you may not feel resentment that they attend too many events.

How to handle friendships in your marriage

Friendships in your marriage come with some challenges, such as:

- learning ways to handle your partner spending alone time with their friends.
- learning how to handle spending time with just your friends
- Learning how to handle your partner spending a lot of alone time with a friend of the opposite sex.
- There could be some jealousy that they spend too much time with friends (especially friends of the opposite gender)

But these challenges don't have to be problematic. So before you and your partner get caught up in clashes and arguments over friends, you have to talk.

- **Start by letting go of your controlling behavior.** You have to understand that you and your spouse are different people. You can't force them to be like you, so you have to be willing to let go of the idea that you can control them. Being controlling is unhealthy and would cause more conflicts and long-term problems in your marriage. Being controlling will make your partner feel frustrated, lonely, and trapped, and would incite him or her to rebel against you. Instead, express your boundaries in clear terms, reach a compromise that satisfies both of you, and see if your partner can respect that.
- **Both of you should figure out the ground rules and expectations in your marriage.** Have you both laid out your boundaries? Have you communicated what is and isn't acceptable to you? Have you explained what constitutes cheating to you? You need to have these conversations because only when you both know the boundaries and rules can you truly respect them.
- **Have an honest dialogue about your needs, expectations and challenges when it comes to maintaining friendships in your marriage.** Speak from a place of acceptance and compassion, do not get defensive. Work towards achieving a social balance in the relationship.
- **Listen very attentively to your spouse's perspective.** Do not downplay your partner's suspicions or fears, telling your partner not to worry about someone who is showing interest in you or who is being mean to them is the opposite of reassuring. Instead, assure them that if someone couldn't respect your marital boundaries, you would walk away from such friendship to protect your relationship. Now that is how you reassure your partner.

SUB-TOPIC 3:

HOW TO MAINTAIN FRIENDSHIPS IN YOUR MARRIAGE

*A*gain, let's look at this scenario:

Bob and Ashley have been married for about eight years now. Ashley had begun complaining for the past few months that she needs more attention from Bob. She feels like he is putting his relationship with his family and friends before her. Bob completely disagrees with her point of view because he sees it from a different light. In his opinion, he gives her his full attention, talks with her constantly, takes her on dates, is vulnerable, honest and open with her and is always appreciating her efforts and presence in his life. He believes she doesn't notice his efforts and is only focused on being grumpy about the time he spends with his family and friends.

The thing is, they both have different personalities. Bob grew up in a tight-knit loving family and enjoys chatting with family members over the phone on a daily basis. He also has a small group of friends and work colleagues that he frequently hangs out with. He is a very extroverted person and makes friends very easily. He enjoys working at his place of work and feels connected with the staff members at his workplace, like they were family.

Meanwhile, Ashley is not as close with her family, and barely has any friends asides the ladies at church, who she doesn't even relate much with. She is self-employed and works from home as a ghost writer.

Now the problem is Bob can't imagine pushing his friends and family away to create extra time to spend with Ashley. He wants to know how he can assure Ashley that she would always come first, and at the same time he needs his circle of family and friends to survive.

The pertinent questions in the above scenario are:

Which relationship has top priority?
Can we nurture both relationships well?
What are the costs of sacrificing either relationship for the other?
Is there a magic formula for relationship success?
Which relationship has top priority?

It's a no-brainer question, of course your marriage takes top priority. From the sample scenario, we see that Bob knows his wife is top priority and is willing to learn the ways he can assure her that she would always come first to him. You see your willingness to keep your partner assured of their place as top priority of your relationship list should never waver.

If your partner expresses insecurity or is upset about how much time you spend with other people frequently, find ways to show your spouse that you love him or her, and that your other connections and friendships will not overthrow your love for them.

How do you achieve this?

- Note that this requires time, attention, and dedication. But it's definitely worth it.
- Make time to be alone together, engage in fun activities and make your partner fall in love with you all over again.
- Prioritize being each other's closest confidant, and prefer each other to everyone else. appreciate your spouse's vulnerability and honesty rather than express frustration or resentment. It's not easy to be vulnerable and be open about how insecure you feel because of the fear of coming off as too needy or clingy. So appreciate your partner's honesty. Your appreciation of their vulnerability and empathetic listening will keep your relationship healthy for better communication.

2. Can we nurture both relationships well?

Yes, you can. There is a correct way to balance and manage both relationships without alienating your partner or sacrificing his or her need to be heard, and cared for. A balance between marital unity and your individuality is important for your happiness long-term.

3. What are the costs of sacrificing either relationship for the other?

You shouldn't sacrifice your marriage to maintain your close friendships and social connections, and you also shouldn't be sacrificing your social connections to appease your marriage. It is important that you have other friendships, otherwise, your number one person becomes the only person in your life. That can get boring. And when you get bored with your partner, your partner becomes less an object of desire and more an object of duty and obligation. I am certain you do not want to resent the fact that you have become each other's entire world. Instead, you want to enjoy sharing ever-broadening aspects of your lives. These broadening aspects are created by the friendships and social connections enjoyed outside of your union. Never forget that maintaining rich and meaningful social connections adds a positive dimension and better perspective to your marriage.

4. Is there a magic formula for relationship success?

Yes, there is. The following steps have been proven to work:

- **Listen:** Allow your spouse explain exactly why they feel the way they feel? Do your best to remain curious, not defensive. When you are defensive, your language and behavior tend to shut down opportunities for deep sharing. Defensiveness also shows that you are not really listening nor taking responsibility for your own part in contributing to the distance in your marriage. The goal of listening is to prioritize your partner and make him or her feel loved and heard. Show that you are committed to working on your relationship.
- **Make informed decisions together:** After listening, use the necessary information you have gathered from your partner to begin setting relationship priorities. Together, both of you should determine which compromises will

need to be made to make your marriage work. What things are you willing to change? Which core relationships can you never give up?
- **Keep the attraction alive in your marriage.** Show your partner that you are committed to having the best of friendships with them. That they are important in your life.
- **Be honest with your partner about what your social connections mean to your couple relationship.** Tell him or her how important it is to you that you both are comfortable with each other's friends. Encourage girls or guys night out, suggest trips with mutual friends or regular double dates. Make conscious efforts to be familiar with each other's friends. So if you have never tried communicating to your spouse how important your social connections are to your life together, then You definitely should.
- **Resist the urge to feel resentment.** It is easy to resent the idea of your spouse having friends outside of your marital connection, but remember that connections outside your marriage are important, nourishing, and strong contributors to your happiness. Resentment is a dangerous thing. It causes negative reactions and emotions in both of you. Do not allow it to become the death of your union.

Why is it important that spouses become comfortable with each other's friends?

Like I had mentioned earlier, couples need to spend some time apart with their own friends, so as to maintain some independence and to nurture their respective friendships. However, just as important as spending time with your friends on your own is including your partner in those group outings, too. But make sure to not force it, you don't want your spouse going out with you grudgingly.

How to help your partner get more comfortable with your friends.

If your spouse is a shy person or is introverted (or maybe your friends are a lot), they may need a little helping hand from you.

Here is how you can help:

- limit the number of people your spouse meets at once. Start in small doses, because it can be very overwhelming for your partner to be introduced to all your friends at once and still be expected to feel as comfortable with them as you are.
- Help by prepping your partner ahead of time on the people they are going to be meeting so they are ready with interesting and engaging conversation starters. Make sure to include things and topics they have a common interest in, this will be of immense help to your spouse when they strike up conversations.
- Set your partner up with those friends that you suspect he or she will connect with the easiest. It seamlessly eases your partner into your friend group when they can connect easily with at least one other friend asides you.

What are the signs that show your spouse is comfortable with your friends?

1. One of the clearest signs that your partner is comfortable with your friends is if he or she takes an active role in spending more time with your friends. If your spouse is asking questions about your friends' well-being and suggesting group outings with them, then he or she feels like they are becoming friends with your friends. And if your partner is suggesting a double date with your other couple friends then you know that he or she actually genuinely enjoys spending time with your friends, and is willing to include them in your precious date nights.
2. Another clear sign is if your partner isn't attached to your hip in a group setting. When you are assured that during hangouts with your friends, your partner won't be sticking to your side like glue throughout the event and panicking whenever you go to the bathroom, then you can be certain that your spouse is comfortable with your friends. Another

indicator is that your partner is able to have independent and animated discussions with your friends during hangouts.
3. The third sign that your spouse is interested in being friends with your friends is if he or she is constantly saying positive things about your friends and compliments them often. This is true because You mostly see the positives in something you genuinely like.
4. The best sign is when you can see that your partner is actually enjoying themselves with your friends. When you can hear a genuine laugh from your spouse, it communicates that they are connecting with your friend and like them. Also when they are enthusiastically engaging in whatever activity that your friends are doing, whether it be dancing, singing, bowling, or playing board games.
5. You can tell your partner is at ease with your friends when he or she makes a conscious effort to engage your friends in conversation, and ask questions to get to know them better. It is a plus if your partner remembers minor details about your friends lives, and details from the convo.

23

PRACTICE EXERCISE

Plan outings with each other's friends: Plan a double date or group friend outing where you invite a few of your partner's friends and a few of your friends. This will help to create fun memories that will make everyone feel more comfortable together.

TOPIC 6:

Codependency

–Unconditional Love

What is codependency? Despite codependency sounding like it would be a positive dynamic in a relationship, it would interest you to find out that **it actually isn't.** In fact, it is the very opposite of positive, it is toxic and unhealthy.

According to the *oxford language dictionary*, codependency is 'the excessive emotional or psychological reliance on a partner, typically one who requires support on account of an illness or addiction'. Another definition is by *Wikipedia* "Codependency is a behavioral condition in a relationship where one person enables another person's addiction, poor mental health, immaturity, irresponsibility, or under-achievement."

It is an emotional and behavioral condition that can impact a person's ability to have a healthy, mutually satisfying relationship. Sometimes, it is referred to as a **relationship addiction.** This is because codependents tend to have one-sided relationships with other people where their own needs and wants come in second or not at all and they are extremely dependent- emotionally, socially and sometimes physically - on the other person (which is characteristic of addiction).

The term **codependency is descriptive of a mostly negative relationship dynamic.** This refers to an unhealthy relationship which people might share with those closest to them.

One of the core characteristics of codependency is an excessive reliance on other people for approval and a sense of identity. Codependency had been originally thought to involve only families of substance abuse [such as alcoholics] but with modern understanding, it has since grown to include other types of dysfunctional relationships.

The idea of codependency proposed in the theories of a German psychoanalyst, Karen Horney, in 1941 is that some people adopt a "moving toward" personality style to overcome their basic anxiety. Essentially, these people basically move toward others by gaining their approval and affection, and then they subconsciously control them through their dependent style.

25

WHO IS A CODEPENDENT PERSON?

A codependent person, in this context, is someone who has an extreme focus outside themselves. Their thoughts and actions revolve around other people, such as spouses, friends or relatives.

Many codependent persons place a lower priority on their own needs, while being excessively preoccupied with the needs of others.

Codependents can also be characterized as being unselfish, virtuous, martyr-like, faithful, and the type to turn the other cheek despite personal humiliation.

Generally, approval from their significant other is more important than their own self-respect.

These are some of the common signs of codependent behavior:

- Taking responsibility for someone else's actions
- Worrying or carrying the burden for others' problems
- Covering up to protect others from reaping the consequences of their poor choices (such as addictions, immaturity, irresponsibility, or under-achievement)
- Doing more than is required at your job or at home to earn approval
- Feeling obligated to do what others expect without consulting one's own needs

- Manipulating others' responses instead of accepting them at face value
- Being suspicious of receiving love, not feeling "worthy" of being loved
- In a relationship based on need, not out of mutual respect
- Trying to solve someone else's problems, or trying to change someone
- Enabling someone to take our time or resources without our consent
- Neglecting their own needs in the process of caring for someone who doesn't want to care for themselves.

So if you do many or even every one of those, then you are most likely a codependent person.

So What causes codependency?

Codependency is often rooted in childhood. Children who grow up in dysfunctional families grow to believe they do not matter and/or they are the cause of the family problems. Dysfunctional families are chaotic, unpredictable, judgmental, secretive, manipulative, unsupported, scary, unsafe, overly harsh and abusive, emotionally and/or physically neglectful. The children are blamed for the problems or are told there is no problem (which can be very confusing for the child because he/she intuitively knows something is wrong, but the adults keep gaslighting and invalidating the child's feelings). The child assumes he/she is the problem, and begins to think he/she is unworthy, stupid, bad, incapable, and the cause of the family dysfunction. These negative thoughts create the roots of adult codependent relationships. The child may believe that his or her needs are not worth attending to, and grow up into a codependent adult. Because growing up in a household where their emotions are ignored or punished gives the child a low self-esteem and constant feeling of shame.

How do you know if you are codependent?

I would need you to answer these questions honestly:

- Are you always worried about other people's opinions of you?

- Do you feel humiliation and embarrassment when your child or spouse makes a mistake?
- Are the opinions of others more important than your own joy?
- Do you feel rejected when significant others spend time with friends?
- Are you uncomfortable expressing your true feelings to others?
- Do you feel like a "terrible person" when you make a mistake?
- Have you ever lived with someone who hits or belittles you?
- Do you think people in your life would go astray and fall apart without your constant efforts?
- Do you have trouble saying "no" when asked for help?

If you answered yes to most of these questions, then you most likely have codependent behavior. However, take note that *only a qualified professional can make a diagnosis of co-dependency*; because not everyone experiencing these symptoms suffers from co-dependency.

How can codependency affect your relationship?

Codependency comes from a place of anxiety. You or your partner want reassurance and you do not want to take any risks. As a result, you base your moods on that of your significant other's because doing so helps you feel safer. Their happiness is literally your only happiness.

Codependency becomes a serious problem when one person starts to feel like they are being suffocated. Or, it can turn bad when one person is constantly sacrificing their own needs to make the other person happy.

Codependency affects people's abilities to have mutually enjoyable relationships. In an attempt to not be selfish, we are less ourselves and more of what others expect us to be and it could lead to over-commitment or abuse.

Several other negatives associated with codependency include distrust, faulty expectations, passive-aggressiveness, controlling attitudes, self-neglect, manipulation, and a bunch of other unattractive traits.

The thing about codependency is that most people claim to fall into it as an inexplicable result of unconditional love. They use 'unconditional love' as an excuse to defend their toxic codependent habits.

This begs the question, **what really is love?**

Different people from different times and places have come up with various conclusions as to what love really is. Love really is a popular word, as old as time itself.

One idea was that love is divine and God is love. Some others objectively thought **love as an intense and profound feeling or an emotional state caused by affection.**

The common idea is that to find true love is to find a good thing and to fill a void in your life.

If great writers from Lawrence Durrell (who said *"to love another person is to see the face of God"*) to Mark Twain (*"love: the irresistible desire to be irresistibly desired"*) all saw love from these varying but essentially similar perspectives then, one can only say that love has many faces among which is **unconditional love.**

When is love said to be unconditional?

Unconditional love is affection without any limitations, or love without conditions. **That is, loving someone unselfishly and regardless of circumstance, not expecting anything in return.**

Unconditional love is said to be the purest form of love there is and synonymous with true love. You don't base it on what someone does for you in return. You simply love them and want nothing more than their overall happiness and peace. Some common examples of it in today's world would be a mother's love for her child and the story of the love of Christ for all of humanity.

A mother would give all she has and more to ensure that her child gets the best. She goes the extra mile to make her child feel safe. The story of King Solomon and two mothers from the Hebrew bible would suffice for a good example.

Want to hear the story? Okay, story time!

There were two women who gave birth around the same time. One night, both of them were fast asleep with their babies by their sides. One of the women, while still deep in sleep, mistakenly rolls on top of her child and kills the baby. She wakes up to realize that her baby is dead, and quickly replaces the dead child with the other woman's living baby. (Evil and mean, I know!)

Now, the other woman wakes up to find a dead child that is not hers lying beside her. She becomes upset and confronts the first woman about it. It leads to a huge argument that is finally brought before the king, King Solomon, to decide who the guilty party was.

King Solomon, a very wise man who understands the emotional depths of a mother's love, asks that the living baby be cut into two halves, with each woman receiving one half each. With this strategy, he was able to recognize the 'false-mother' as the woman who enthusiastically approved of his proposal, while the actual mother of the living baby begged and cried that the sword be taken away and the living baby be given to her rival instead. The real mother would rather watch her child be raised by another woman, than see the baby die before her eyes.

In that very moment, all she cared about was the well-being of her child. she was more than willing to sacrifice her pride and her need to prove that she was the wronged party in that issue. She didn't care about being 'right' anymore, and didn't mind seeing her rival raise her baby if it meant her baby would live. She wasn't going to let all the sacrifices and pain she went through before and during childbirth go to waste because of a moment of pride. This is characteristic of unconditional love. This above story is an example of the unconditional love of a mother for her child.

The ending? King Solomon, of course, gave her baby back to her. He recognized the compassion in her eyes and body language as that of a mother's. And she got to live happily ever after with her child.

We often associate unconditional love with familial love, because it brings to mind the love your parents have for you or the love you have for your own child. Many of us search actively for this type of love in romantic relationships. It is an understandable desire, we all want someone to love us for who we are, no matter what. We've sung about it, dream about it, watched movies about it, read books about it, and really just want to find it.

What unconditional love is:

- It gives a warm and secure feeling. Unconditional love provides a sense of security in both childhood and adulthood. When you are confident in someone's love and know it won't go away (even after you make mistakes, have different life goals, have a life-altering health condition or changes in appearance), it would help create secure attachments and foster autonomy, independence, and greater self-worth. Knowing you are loved no matter what makes you feel secure about yourself and your place in life.
- Unconditional love involves healthy boundaries. Even when offering unconditional love to the subject of your affection (even when they are being difficult or stubborn), you don't have to offer love without bounds. You can offer love that has no strings attached while still having boundaries.

What unconditional love isn't:

- Ignoring relationship issues. Unconditional love does not mean you avoid conflict or look away from problematic behavior. Do not ignore problematic behavior and toxic environments on the basis of unconditional love, cos that is not what unconditional love is.
- Neglecting your own needs. It is true that unconditional love involves sacrifice and being selfless, but these sacrifices should not require you giving up on everything you need and want for yourself. You should be able to set boundaries around things you don't want to do, and your lover should respect your limits.
- Tolerating abuse. unconditional love does not mean staying in an unhealthy situation when you are better off leaving. Do not put up with a person that verbally abuses and physically assaults you on the grounds of unconditional love. You can offer forgiveness and love, even after leaving the relationship. You might not ever stop loving them, but neither should you ignore the abuses.

How can unconditional love go wrong?

Unconditional love starts to go wrong when the lover becomes codependent and starts enabling bad behaviors in their beloved. Or when on multiple occasions, the lover endangers themselves to enable their beloved. Once this happens, you are veering away from the fresh springs of true unconditional love and diving into the murky waters of codependency.

Another issue has been with people developing Stockholm syndrome and confusing it with unconditional love. Stockholm syndrome is a psychological response that occurs when hostages or abuse victims' bond with their captors or abusers.

For example, people who are taken hostage often feel threatened by their captor, but they are also highly reliant on them for survival. If the kidnapper or abuser shows them some kindness, they may begin to feel positive feelings toward their captor for this "compassion".

Over time, that perception begins to reshape and distort how they view the person keeping them hostage or abusing them.

What are the Ways to overcome codependency?

Codependent relationships are generally unhealthy, but this doesn't mean the relationship is doomed. It just means that it is going to take some work and conscious efforts to get things back on track. The following are recommended ways to overcome codependency:

Consider A Therapy.

If you are struggling with this complicated issue, I advise that you seek help from a therapist who has experience working with recovery from codependency.

Therapy would help you:

1. Identify your codependent behavior patterns and guide you in taking steps to deal with.
2. Challenge your negative thought patterns
3. Work on increasing your self-esteem.

Therapy is necessary because codependent habits and traits can become so entrenched in a person's personality and behavior that the person might have a hard time recognizing them on his or her own.

And even when they are recognized, codependency can be tough to overcome on your own.

B. Love yourself deeply and completely.

"To Love Oneself Is the Beginning of a Lifelong Romance." - Oscar Wilde

You may have heard that it is unhealthy to make your life all about your partner, and this is true. You need friends, hobbies, and other interests besides your partner to balance yourself out. Relying too much on your partner to fulfill all your needs can burn a relationship out, and frankly, it is unfair to your partner.

You need to take care of yourself so that your relationship becomes the cherry on top of the cake, as opposed to the whole cake. Once you ensure that your own needs have been met, then you have a much better chance of seeing your relationship blossom into one that is respectful and filled with unconditional love.

C. Set boundaries for yourself.

A boundary is a limit you set around things you are not comfortable with. To be real, if you are dealing with long-standing codependency, boundaries are not always easy to set or stick to. You might be so familiar with making others comfortable that you have a hard time considering your own limits.

It would take some practice before you can get used to and repeatedly honor your own boundaries, but these tips can help:

- Practice polite refusals. Examples are "I'm sorry, but I'm not free at the moment", "Thank you for the invite, but I'd rather not tonight. maybe another time."
- Question your motive before you do something for anybody: ask yourself the following questions: "What are the reasons I am doing this?" "Do I want to or do I feel I have to?" "If I do this, will I still have energy to meet my own needs after?"
- Listen to the other person's problems with empathy, but don't offer solutions or try to fix it for them, unless you are involved with the problem.

D. Offer healthy support.

When your partner has some problems, there is nothing wrong with wanting to help him or her, but there are ways to do so without sacrificing your own needs. They are:

1. Listening to your partner's worries or problems
2. Discussing possible solutions with them, rather than for them. Remember don't charge over their lives or bear their problems for them. Offer suggestions and advice only when asked
3. Stepping back to let them make their own decision. Give them the space to be their own person, don't try to manage or direct their behavior or choices.
4. Offering compassion and acceptance of whatever choices they make for their lives.

E. Practice valuing yourself

Oftentimes, Codependency and low self-esteem are linked together. If you link your self-worth to your ability to care for others, developing a sense of self-worth that does not depend on your relationships with other people can be challenging and hard.

An increased self-worth leads to increased self-esteem, increased confidence and happiness. All of these are important because it makes it easier for you to express your needs and set boundaries, both of which are important tools in overcoming codependency. The following tips will set you on the right path to having an increased sense of self-worth:

1. Spend time with people who treat you well. surround yourself with positive people who value you and offer acceptance and support. Consistently limit the time spent with people who say or do things that make you feel bad about yourself, and drain your energy.
2. Let go of the negative self-talks. If you tend to criticize yourself, re-frame these negative thought patterns to affirm yourself instead. You are smart, beautiful and courageous, don't ever think less of yourself.
3. Do things you enjoy. Try setting aside some time each day

to do things that make you happy, whether it's reading a book, singing, knitting, dancing, playing games, watching a movie. The time you have spent looking after others may have kept you from exploring hobbies or other interests, now it is time to invest that time in yourself. Doing things, you enjoy will help you gain back your confidence and happiness.

F. Balance is key —create some autonomy.

In forming a positive and balanced relationship, people in codependent relationships may need to take small steps toward some separation in the relationship. How to do that:

1. Find a hobby: The codependent person may need to find a hobby or activity they enjoy doing outside of the relationship.
2. The enabler must also recognize that they are not helping their codependent partner by allowing them to make extreme sacrifices.
3. Individual or group therapy is also very helpful for people who are in codependent relationships. An expert can help them find ways to acknowledge and express their feelings that may have been unhealthily suppressed since childhood.

These steps are not easy to take but are worth the effort to help both of you discover how to be in a balanced relationship.

AFTERWORD

Codependency is a mostly negative relationship dynamic that is characterized by an excessive reliance on other people for approval and a sense of identity. Meanwhile unconditional love is affection given without any conditions, it is loving someone unselfishly and regardless of circumstance, not expecting anything in return. The major difference is that Codependency is unhealthy and Unconditional love is healthy. However, be careful that your unconditional love does not stray off its right path into the toxic way of Codependency.

TOPIC 7:

Love Language

–Desire Discrepancy

What is love language? Have you ever heard of the five love languages? It has become a very popular concept since it was first introduced and developed in 1992 by Dr. Gary Chapman in the book *"The Five Love Languages: How to Express Heartfelt Commitment to Your Mate"*.

According to him, everyone in spite of the difference in their life experiences and varying personalities ultimately gives and receives love in 5 different ways. He termed them the five love languages. Under this framework, each person has **at least one** language that they prefer above the other. And it is possible to learn to "speak" all five love languages.

The Definition: Love language (or the language of love as I like to call it) is the way you express your feelings of love toward someone, or something you love, and the way you prefer to be loved.

You must have heard a person or two say "he or she speaks my love language" or "words of affirmation is my love language".

So, what are the five love languages?

They are:

1. Words of Affirmation
2. Quality Time
3. Receiving Gifts
4. Acts of Service
5. Physical Touch

WORDS OF AFFIRMATION

They are verbal statements that display affection. It consists of compliments, heartfelt declarations of love, romantic statements and texts, expressions of pride and appreciation. People with words of affirmation as a love language value verbal acknowledgments of affection.

How to know if words of affirmation is your love language:

- You get an excited thrill from receiving compliments and unexpected praise
- You enjoy when others say they care about you or appreciate having you in their lives
- You love feeling understood and appreciated
- You like receiving recognition for a job well done.

If your spouse's primary love language is words of affirmation, your spoken praises and appreciation will make him or her feel loved and happy. **Here is how you can express your love using words of affirmation,** thereby keeping your spouse's love tank full:

- Be Encouraging and Empathetic: Consistently express your support and understanding of your partner's successes and their struggles.
- Express Your Admiration often: Give compliments frequently. Do it privately, do it publicly, and do it consistently. Your partner will be glad because of your efforts and feel loved.
- Compliment, don't criticize: if a person's love language is "words of affirmations," then hurling an insult or hurtful criticisms will hurt that person more than it might hurt another person. There is a fine line between those words of affirmation that are intended as suggestions and those that

will be interpreted as demands. Be sure to always keep your words loving and offer guidance, not give ultimatums.
- Write and leave love notes around the house: Nothing says romance like Love Notes. Those written reminders of your love will go a long way in making your spouse feel loved. Place the love notes in places they can view it easily. Also, sending cute flirty texts and emails would do the trick also.
- Be Vocal in Bed: Yes, please. Expressing your pleasures and desires during intimate moments lets your lover know how good they make you feel, and in turn helps them to feel more loved.
- Learn a broad range of compliments: If finding the right phrase and compliments doesn't always come easy to you, then broaden your vocabulary by listening for affirming words during your daily life. Note these complimentary terms you hear, then work them into your own love language.

27

QUALITY TIME

Quality time as a love language centers around togetherness. It is all about expressing your love and affection for your spouse with your undivided attention. When you are with your partner, you put away any distractions (put down your cell phone, turn off the tablet, close the laptop) and focus on them. When you do that, it touches their heart in a way that makes them feel important, loved, and special. The thought that you were intentional in setting aside time just for them makes them happy and loved. For a person whose primary love language is quality time, a lack of connectedness can leave them feeling empty and alone.

How to know if quality time is your love language:

- You feel loved when your partner makes time for you in their schedule,
- You are thrilled when your partner clears their whole schedule to dedicate the whole period in hanging out with you.
- You love spending time with your lover and especially love it when he or she pays undivided attention to you and you alone.

Now, if your partner's primary love language is quality time, you would need to learn to speak this language fluently. If your love language is different from your partner's, your efforts at being adept in their language may seem a little unnatural to you at first, but push on and you will be fluent in no time. Here's **how you can express your love using quality time:**

- Make and maintain eye contact: By maintaining eye contact, you are communicating to your partner that they have your full attention and that you care about what they have to say. This will make them feel loved, important, and understood.
- Actively listen to your spouse's thoughts: Focus on what they are saying, you might even lean in slightly. affirm what they are saying and ask thoughtful questions. Also, avoid trying to offer advice, unless they ask for it. Your partner is more interested in feeling understood and looking for your empathy and compassion.
- Put away distractions: Make it a habit to put away every distraction at dinner or during a coffee break and really focus on what your partner has to say. Even though you may not be discussing anything earth-shattering, you are at least making an important and loving gesture by choosing your partner over everything else. It hurts a quality time person deeply when they share something that is important to them, only to look up and realize that their partner is only half paying attention and is distracted by the TV or is discreetly trying to answer an email from a coworker.
- Focus on the quality of the time spent together and not the amount of time used. The quality of your interactions count, focus on enjoying one another's company. Stay in the moment and enjoy the richness of each other's company.
- Take steps to initiate quality time together. This will mean a lot to your partner and would communicate to him or her that you love spending time with them. It would also assure them that you don't think they are being clingy or needy, because you want to spend time with them too.

28

RECEIVING GIFTS

The act of gift giving is often the most misconstrued love language. Many think it seems greedy, or that the receiver is fixated on material things rather than love itself. This is actually not the case.

The true meaning of gift giving is not extravagance, it is sentimentality. It communicates to your partner that "I was thinking about you when I saw this. You're always on my mind." Every time they see the gifted item, it will serve as a reminder that they are loved.

If your spouse's primary love language is receiving gifts, you will make him or her feel loved and treasured by giving gifts on birthdays, anniversaries, days of promotions and achievements, holidays and even on random days. Receiving gifts is the thing that makes them feel loved most deeply.

The gifts do not have to be expensive or elaborate. Something as simple as a homemade card or a few cheerful flowers will communicate your love to your spouse. Little things mean a lot to a person whose primary love language is receiving gifts, it is the thought that counts to them.

How to know if receiving gifts is your love language:

- You are highly enthusiastic when you are receiving gifts and put the item on display, or wear it every day, or gush to your friends about it

- You feel very loved at the gesture of receiving gifts.
- You always have an arsenal of wrapping paper and gift bags for all occasions.
- You have a tough time getting rid of gifts you have received, even after decades.
- You take pride in picking the perfect, personalized gifts for every occasion.

Here is how you can express your love by giving gifts: It's simple, give gifts. You could stop at a pastry and buy delicious treats for your partner before heading home. You could pick out pretty flowers for them.

Make them thoughtful, make them sweet, splurge on grand extravagant gifts whenever you can. Your gifts do not have to be big purchases, and they do not have to be everyday. But they should come frequently enough to remind your partner that they are always on your mind.

29
ACTS OF SERVICE

*A*cts of Service as a Love language can best be described as doing something for your partner that you know they would like, things such as watering their plants, assisting them with house chores, doing their laundry, or cooking them a meal.

If acts of service is your spouse's primary love language, nothing will speak more deeply to him or her emotionally than simple acts of service.

- **Pay attention to the small things and act accordingly:** pay attention to the minor details such as what time your partner's favorite show is on, what their favorite brands are, how much sugar he or she adds to their morning coffee, etc. Take notes of these preferences and do things they would like while paying attention to these details. So if you go grocery shopping, you could buy items from their preferred brands. You could prepare their coffee exactly how they like it in the mornings. You could tune in to their favorite show when it's on.
- **Focus on those acts of service that are easy for you to accommodate into both your schedules.** Pay attention to both your calendars each week and see how you can fit in Acts of Service. So if your lover has little time each day to get ready for work after their morning workouts, plan to

have coffee and breakfast ready and waiting so they don't have to rush to work hungry. Or you could help service and wash your partner's car during the weekend.
- **Pay attention to the things your partner doesn't enjoy doing and help out.** If your spouse complains about taking out the trash or walking the dog, then you can do these tasks for your partner. Offer your services whenever you can do something your partner struggles with.

30

PHYSICAL TOUCH

*P*hysical touch as a love language is not all about sex, although sex is a part of it. Desiring physical touch is usually more about feeling seen and safe than it is about intercourse. It includes both intimate and non-intimate touches, and it shows a preference for physical expressions of love over all other expressions.

Physical touch are the hugs, kisses, foot massage, the back rubs before you fall asleep, a shoulder squeeze, a handhold, a pat on the back. For those whose love language is physical touch, for them it is so soothing, warm, and reassuring to be touched.

How to know if physical touch is your love language:

- You are comfortable with public displays of affection, even in front of a crowd.
- You would feel lonely in the relationship if you were not able to express or receive physical affection.
- You love giving hugs and sitting close to others.
- You are usually looking forward to kisses and intimacy with your partner more than anything else.
- You like to get massages on a regular basis and love the occasional foot rub.

Here's **how you can express your love using physical touch:**

- Kissing: Kissing is one of the easiest, most effective ways to show physical love to your partner. You can kiss their lips, their neck, their cheek, their forehead, their hand.
- Cuddling: Physically wrapping yourself around your partner can bring you two closer together, physically and emotionally. Try swapping roles between being the 'big spoon' and the 'little spoon', or facing each other and seeing how that feels.
- Holding hands: when you hold hands with your partner, whether in public or in private, it is an easy gesture that can immediately release mood-boosting endorphins.
- Skin-to-skin touching: this is an expressive way of telling your partner you are physically attracted to them, you are there for them, and you are in love with them. Examples of skin-to-skin touching is foot rubs, back massages, rubbing their backs, touching your partner's hair, dragging your fingertips across their back or neck, touching their bare legs.
- Sitting side-by-side: Sitting with your hips or feet touching is a non-verbal way of connecting with your partner and communicating that you love them.

31

PRIMARY AND SECONDARY LOVE LANGUAGES

It is possible to have just one main love language. It is also possible to have more than one —a mix of two or more, or even qualities from all five languages.

According to Dr. Chapman, everybody has a primary and secondary love language. Your primary love language is the one that resonates "love" to you the most. Your secondary love language has less intensity compared to your primary love language, but it still communicates love to you. Your primary love languages may be words of affirmation and physical touch, while your secondary love language may be receiving gifts. This means, you appreciate compliments, hearing 'I love you' frequently, and having physical contacts with your lover the most, but you also feel loved when you receive an unexpected gift.

So what do you think your primary and secondary love languages are? Figure it out, so you can communicate better to your spouse the ways you love to be loved.

The two sides of Love Languages –Giving and Receiving.

it is possible to give out a different love language(s) than you prefer to receive. This is the extra layer of complexity that we must take into consideration. How you instinctively give love may not be the same as how you receive love. For some people, their giving and receiving love languages align i.e. they give out and take in the same love language(s). But for some others, this is not the case. And this is perfectly normal. For example, you may enjoy giving and surprising your loved ones with gifts, but you do not enjoy receiving them and especially dislike surprises.

To avoid problems arising from this complexity, you can alter the way you give love to match how your partner receives love. That way you will see an improvement in your relationship.

How do you know what your partner's love language is?

- **By Observing and Recognizing:** One way is to take a step back and observe keenly how your spouse expresses his or her love to you. maybe your partner expresses their love for you by bringing home your favorite snacks or calling during work breaks. Then you can recognize that they love giving out Gifts and Quality Time as a love language.

But because of the complexity with love languages that I mentioned earlier, about how the way you give love may not be the same as how you would prefer to receive love. So the next method of knowing your partner's love language is the best:

- **Through Honest and Open Communication:** just ask your spouse. It would save you from speculating and guessing wrong. Have in-depth discussions with your partner about the ways in which you both like to express and receive love. Try asking open-ended questions about what kinds of words or actions indicate love for your partner, and how they like to express their love for you. Also see if you can learn why they have a particular love language, where it might come from, and what it means for them (physically and emotionally). This would help give all the information you need to know about your partner's love language.

Having a different love language from your partner's?

Many of the problems a lot of couples face is because they feel and express love in different ways.

In many cases, Love languages stem from your upbringing and childhood experiences. Perhaps while growing up, your parents routinely hugged and kissed you in the morning or late night before going to bed and told you how much they love you (Physical Touch, Words of Affirmation).

Or maybe they showed their love by always driving you personally to and from school and cheering you on each time (Acts of Service, Quality Time). Or they showered you with gifts and toys while growing up (Gifts).

Depending on whichever style your parents used overtime, you may have also adopted these love languages as your own.

Now that you are grown and, in a relationship, your partner may not recognize your acts as an expression of love or/and does not reciprocate it either, because their Love Language differs from yours. Then there is going to be a miscommunication and both of you might not feel loved because you are not being loved the right way.

But by learning the grammar of your different love languages, you can improve your communication with your spouse and increase the love.

An example scenario is this:

Kira has been married to Liam for 3 years now. She was frustrated with her marriage and decided to go for couples counseling in a last bid to save her marriage. When asked by Dr. Temi, their marriage counselor, what she felt the issue was, Kira replies "Everyday, Liam tells me he loves me, but he never does anything to help me. I do most of the house chores and he just sit on the couch playing games on his PS4. The thought never crosses his mind to assist me, except I ask. I'm tired of asking to be helped, he should know he should without my pleadings. If he loved me, I wouldn't have to remind him to assist me in the house chores. I'm just really sick of hearing I love you when the actions don't match the words!"

You see Kira's primary love language is acts of service (not words of affirmation), and even though her husband, Liam, loved her, he had not been expressing his love in a way that made her feel loved.

However, after counseling, Liam learn to speak Kira's love language and their marriage blossomed.

32

DESIRE DISCREPANCY
WHAT IS DESIRE DISCREPANCY?

Breaking the words down to 'desire' and 'discrepancy', desires are simply what a person truly wants. They could be emotional, romantic or sexual. All of which the individual really has little or no control over.

Discrepancy on the other hand is simply the difference between facts.

So basically, desire discrepancy is the difference between one's expected desire styles (or love languages) and what they are actually getting. That is, having one's desire styles unmatched by a counterpart.

A really basic way to look at it is that there is someone who loves PDA (public displays of affection) and someone who doesn't. So there will always be someone who is more open to all sorts of kissing, smooching and groping in public places and someone who is probably not as open to that. That difference of PDA being one's desire style and not the other's is what desire discrepancy is.

This difference might cause couples to question the depth and strength of their love for each other, and either (or both of them) may feel uncared for which can ultimately lead to a physical or emotional disconnection between them. **A major form of desire discrepancy is sexual desire discrepancy (SDD).**

Sexual desire discrepancy (SDD) is the difference between one's desired frequency of sexual intercourse and the actual frequency of sexual intercourse within a relationship. Simply put, one partner wants sex more frequently yet the actual occurrence of sexual intercourse doesn't match that desire. This is a common area of conflict for many couples, it is so common that it is one of the top reasons people seek marriage counseling.

Our sexual needs tend to change over time as we age and our relationship matures. This is completely normal during the course of even the best of relationships. Many couples, as it turns out, actually have experienced some challenges around sexual compatibility.

A lot of people in relationships can relate to these words: "When we first met we could not get enough of each other, but now things are so very different."

The good news is, there are ways to navigate through desire discrepancies, so you don't have to give up on having a fulfilling sexual life.

What are the ways to navigate desire discrepancy in long term relationships?

- Communication,
- Listening attentively
- Negotiations (Making adjustments that would please both of you.)

Communication is key in navigating desire discrepancy. It is important to communicate what you are ready for, so that your partner knows what your sexual desires are like, what you want in the bedroom.

Communication also allows you to know what you both want from your sex lives and the number of times you both could have sex given your schedules, energy level, and emotional capacity at this stage.

Before you start communicating, make sure to create an environment where you both feel safe —like a pillow talk. It is okay if you are feeling some fear or anxiety about discussing sex. It may feel very awkward —to be honest, it often is. And you might find yourselves wondering if you could both pull through the conversation. But, if the energy between you feels safe, and you keep your tone gentle and nonjudgmental, you may be more successful than you hoped. Remember to keep your tone gentle, you will build trust better that way. Do not use judgmental words, because by blaming or criticizing your spouse you can't make any progress. If the idea of navigating through these conversations seems really daunting and emotionally tasking to you, you should visit a marriage counselor together with your spouse. Marriage counselors create the right and safest environment to have these open and honest conversations.

Listen attentively to what your partner is saying. It is very important that you are patient with your partner as they work to find the right words to express themselves. Have you ever been in situations where you struggled to find the perfect words to express yourself? We all have. So be empathetic, put yourself in his/her shoes, and exercise patience. Also, do not plan your responses before your spouse has finished sharing his/her perspectives. Be patient, listen to what he/she has to say, with openness.

Negotiations. Through negotiations, you can state what you are open to, and deconstruct expectations that you can't meet up to. Always look for common ground where you and your partner are both comfortable in. Reach a common ground on the number of times you both could have sex in a week (or month) given your schedules, energy level, and emotional capacity at the moment. It is important that you know there is no "right" number of times to have sex, other than what you both have decided will work for you as a couple.

33
PRACTICAL EXERCISES

- Take a love language test together, to determine your individual love languages.
- Spend time together to write down what you both think are your individual primary love language. Then, list the other four languages in their order of importance for each of you.
- Given your spouse's love language, discuss new exciting ways and renewed past actions you can take to make your spouse feel more loved, cherished and significant
- Now it is your turn, discuss different actions your spouse can take to fill up your love tank and keep you in love.

AFTERWORD

No individual love language is superior to the others. It is ideal that you speak all five languages to your spouse but prioritize and perfect their preferred language.

It may take a few conversations to fully understand your partner's love languages, and it will take practice and patience to put those expressions of love into practice, but the end result of feeling loved and secure in your relationship is worth the effort

TOPIC 8:

Sexuality

–Erotic Blueprints

While researching this particular topic, I found it very eye-opening, I hope you will too.

From the topic, you probably already figured this topic would be about sex.

First things first, **what is sexuality?**

Sexuality has to do with the way you identify, how you experience sexual and romantic attraction (if you do), and your interest in and preferences around sexual and romantic relationships and behavior. Simply put, it is about your sexual feelings, thoughts, attractions and behaviors towards other people.

Sexuality is diverse and personal, and it is an important part of who you are.

According to Jaiya Ma, a world-renowned somatic sexologist, every allosexual (those who experience sexual attraction) regardless of sexuality belongs to one (or more) of five different categories which she termed 'Erotic Blueprints'.

WHAT ARE EROTIC BLUEPRINTS?

A blueprint refers to how a person is wired, therefore, an "erotic" blueprint refers to how a person is sexually wired – their sexual needs, responses, and desires. Your Erotic Blueprint is basically your whole erotic personality.

You could also think of your Erotic Blueprint as your sexual language. Your sexual language communicates what you need to get really aroused (your turn-on), your sexual preferences, how you respond sexually and what your sexual desires are.

Just the same way people with the same personality types share certain attributes, is the same way there are erotic personality types that makes some people prefer super romantic sex, while some deeply enjoy BDSM. Learning and discovering your own and your partner's Erotic Blueprints can help you expand the erotic passion you feel in your relationship and create a deeper sexual connection.

According to Jaiya, your erotic Blueprint is born from a combination of your genetic makeup and how you were brought up. For example, those who were provided with lots of touch and sensations as kids are more likely to be deeply connected with their bodies and are more conditioned towards the Sensual type CEB (Core Erotic Blueprint)

Luckily, although we all have a core blueprint, we are able to create new wiring thereby expanding our expressions of our own sexuality.

WHAT ARE THE 5 EROTIC BLUEPRINTS?

The five erotic personality types are:
   #1: ENERGETIC
#2: SENSUAL
#3: SEXUAL
#4: KINKY
#5: SHAPESHIFTER

#1. ENERGETIC

This erotic personality type is turned on from anticipation, tease, not being touched as much and lots of space.

- They are highly sensitive and live in the realm of emotions.
- For them, anticipation is more arousing than actual sexual touch.
- Also, the more pleasure their lover feels the more aroused they become.

Positive aspect: They are highly sensitive and easily orgasmic, they are turned-on by energy play and by their partner's pleasure.

Shadow aspect: they are affected easily by negative emotions or thoughts; they are more interested in being out of their body

Aroused by: Energy plays, anticipation, their partner's arousal

#2. SENSUAL

They are turned on by lots of touch, smell, aesthetics, beauty and closeness. They want to feel bodies next to each other.

- They are interested in slowing down and being romantic
- They are highly sensual people affected by smell, sound, sight, taste and touch.
- They need to relax before they can have sex

Positive aspect: they are highly sensual in nature, they bring color to sexual experiences, they love to give and receive sensual plays.

Shadow aspect: Stuck in their head, tend to want perfection, they sometimes find it hard to let go.

Aroused by: Sensation play, activities that help them relax (like baths, massages, cuddles), reminders of pleasure throughout their day.

#3. SEXUAL

*O*ur culture often hails this type as the standard, and what it expects men to be as well. They are ready to have sex whenever there is time or a willing partner.

- The opposite of a Sensual type, because while Sensual need to relax before they can have sex, Sexual have sex in order to relax.
- They are easy to turn on by visual or touch stimulus

Positive aspect: They are fun to play with in bed, sexual techniques work well with them, they are easily turned on, Ability to go from aroused to orgasm really quick.

Shadow aspect: They are sometimes oblivious and self-focused during sex, they focus so much on achieving an orgasm that they miss the journey to the orgasm itself.

Aroused by: Nudity, pornography, sex techniques, genital focus, experiencing an orgasm, sexual variety, seeing an erection or a woman's wetness.

#4. KINKY

They are all about turn-on that are taboo. If they do not have a supportive partner who deeply listens to their needs, they can suppress their type and become distant.

- Kinky-wired people are most turned on by "out-of-the-box" sexual encounters.
- They enjoy variety and creativity in sexual play.

Positive aspect: They are turned on by psychological play only, they usually have a rich fantasy life, they enjoy experiencing sexual freedom and extraordinary sexual experiences.

Shadow aspect: They often feel shame or guilt that overrides their desires, they may confuse fantasy with what they really want to experience in real life, they may get stuck in a particular fantasy that becomes their only way to orgasm.

Aroused by: Sexual plays that fit into their specific fantasy, sexual plays that are out of their personal 'norm'

#5. SHAPESHIFTER

*S*hape-Shifters can play in all the types with ease and joy. Some Shape-Shifters are naturally this way and others learn how to wire themselves to be able to play with anyone.

- Sexually sophisticated
- They desire variety

Positive aspect: They are endlessly creative, sexually sophisticated, they can adapt to every erotic blueprint type

Shadow aspect: sometimes they shift to be what others want them to be instead of owning their own sexuality, needs and desires.

Why do you need to identify your Erotic Blueprint?

- So that you can know what turns you on. If you have no idea what turns you on, you can't expect your partner to be able to mind-read your desires and satisfy you.
- It helps you and your partner to better understand how you respond sexually and what your sexual desires are.
- You will no longer feel a sexual disconnect with your partner because he or she will finally understand your sexual language and would be better equipped now to meet your sexual needs.

- you will be able to expand the erotic passion you feel in your relationship and achieve a fulfilling sexual life.

Can you have more than one erotic Blueprint?

Of course, you can be a combination of two or more blueprints. In reality, people actually tend to have a primary and secondary core wiring.

What if we have different erotic Blueprints?

Having different erotic blueprints does not mean your relationship is doomed. It just means your relationship will require that the both of you learn each other's sexual languages. Being fluent in each other's sexual languages will guarantee a much better sex life.

Let me tell you a story:

Nina and Thomas have been married 7 years now, and have a 2-year old son together. From the moment their son had been born, they had struggled sexually —they barely had sex. Nina got frustrated day after day at the fact that Thomas was rejecting her as he fell asleep every night, falling to the bed in exhaustion from taking care of their baby and his day job. She tried often to initiate sex, approaching it from her own blueprint. You see, she was a Sexual, so she would approach him directly by firmly grabbing his genitals while seductively asking "want to have sex?" or climb atop him first thing in the mornings and announce "we've got some time, let's f*ck".

He was always turned off by her bold and direct approach because his blueprint was different, he was a Sensual, he craved mystery and gentle romance. He liked to be cuddled, slowly seduced with sexy lingerie and romantic scents in a sexually-charged ambiance. And that is how he approached her; from his own blueprint. And oh boy! The miscommunication caused by speaking two different languages!

Thomas always tried to initiate sex by snuggling with Nina. But to her, snuggling was not a turn on and rather just a comfortable sleeping position. So, she usually misinterpreted his approach as him wanting to fall asleep. The strain in their sexual life-built resentment in them both. Thomas thought his wife was being petty and refusing to have sex because he could not get turned on by her approach. While Nina thought her husband had lost his sexual drive and feared she was doomed to a sexless marriage. Neither she nor her husband were pleased with their sex life.

Following the advice of a family friend and after the strain in their sex life was beginning to damage their marriage, they finally began seeing a sex therapist. And finally, during their first counseling session, they were introduced to the Erotic Blueprints. They realized then that it wasn't that they were sexually incompatible, they just had different erotic blueprints. In subsequent sessions, they were taught the ways they could learn to enjoy a satisfying sex life despite their different sexual languages. And now, their sex life is as vibrant as their honeymoon phase and very much exciting.

The above scenario begs the question 'how then do we enjoy a satisfying sex life despite having different erotic blueprints?'

How to enjoy satisfying sex despite having different Erotic Blueprints

Learn: You can enjoy satisfying sex by learning yours and your partner's sexual languages.

Communicate: Keep open and honest communication alive, constantly opening up about your needs and desires will help your partner understand you better. It is important to communicate what you are ready for, so that your partner knows what your sexual desires are like, and what you want in the bedroom.

Don't be shy now: It is understandable that you may be feeling shyness or anxiety about discussing sex. It may feel very awkward — to be honest, it sometimes is. But you need to get over that awkwardness and start learning to say and do the things that will up your sex game.

Listen: Listen without judgment to your spouse's needs and desires, especially if your partner has a kinky erotic blueprint. Your judgment might cause your lover to withdraw from the conversation and become distant. It is important that you listen attentively to what he or she is saying. Listen with the intention of understanding their point of view. Be patient and don't interrupt your partner as he or she works to find the right words to express their desires.

Discover together: together, explore your erotic blueprints and realize exciting orgasms. It is best that you both communicate what you each want from your sex lives and the number of times you both could have sex given your schedules, energy level, and emotional capacity at this stage. That way, you have a definite structure and timetable to guide your explorations.

Understand your shadow side: learn what your shadow sides are so that you can avoid them or work through them. Do not be scared to confront this part of your sexuality, find the courage to overcome and conquer it.

Appreciate the differences in your erotic blueprints: when you learn to appreciate each other's differences, you discover the true joy of intimacy.

Why is a fulfilling sexual life important for my marriage?

- Orgasms are beneficial for your health and longevity
- You get a hot steamy marriage instead of one that is stale, boring or mediocre
- Orgasms boost your mood and significantly lowers pain
- When you are sexually alive you have more charisma and attract positivity
- Being Sexually alive equals overall vitality and vibrancy
- You can use sexual energy to awaken or trigger your creativity

42
PRACTICE EXERCISE

To find out your own erotic blueprint and that of your spouse, take Jaiya's free erotic blueprint test. Simply browse the Internet for the erotic blueprint test, and visit missjaiya.com, you should find it quite easily.

AFTERWORD

You can vastly improve your sex life by unlocking your erotic blueprint.

Every erotic blueprint is distinct and unique. They are based around a complex combination of thoughts, images, behaviors, emotions and fantasies. They help to identify who we are, but they do not define who we are. You are not defined by your sexual language. With this knowledge in mind, it is easier to understand how erotic languages works. Know that the more you are able to understand what arouses you, and what really turns you on during sex, the better your sexual experience is going to be.

AFTERWORD

I hope this workbook was as exciting to read, as it was as fun to write.

It is my wish that you fully understand these lessons and put them into practice.

I assure you that putting these lessons into practice in your marriage will give you the union you have always dreamed and hoped for.

By way of reviewing the topics treated in this book, here are the highlights:

TOPIC 1:
HOW WE CONNECT EMOTIONALLY–EMOTIONAL INTELLIGENCE

*E*motional intelligence is key to bonding better with your spouse and achieving a beautiful and long-lasting marriage. It is the awareness of your actions and feelings – and how they affect those around you. It also means that you value others, listen to their wants and needs, and are able to empathize or identify with them on many different levels. Its advantages are numerous, and it will help you get through life on a smooth sail.

TOPIC 2:

THE FOUNDATIONS OF A DIALOGUE–A HONEST COMMUNICATION

The foundation of every dialogue in marriage should be based on honest communication. Both parties should always seek to understand the other's point of view. Do not assume what the other person is saying, make sure to ask instead, let the person clarify. Because oftentimes, assumptions lead to more misunderstandings. Endeavor to always keep communication kind, patient and respectful. Put in the effort to be open and honest with your spouse, because this will increase your relationship satisfaction and bring you two closer together.

TOPIC 3:
APPRECIATIONS AND GRATITUDE–SCARCITY AND ABUNDANCE

*A*ppreciation and Gratitude is fundamentally to every healthy relationship, you and your spouse must work hard to adopt it as part of your lifestyle.

As Les Parrott, a #1 New York Times bestselling author of several marriage advice books, says, "Gratitude can transform common days into Thanksgivings, turn routine jobs into joy, and change ordinary opportunities into blessings."

So choose gratitude and appreciation always! And watch your marriage blossom and bloom.

TOPIC 4:
NEGOTIATION AND COMPROMISE–THE DIFFERENT VALUES

"*I'd do anything in my power to see you just smile*"
The above line was sung in the hit song, smile by the late Jarad Anthony Higgins, famously known as Juice World.

This profession of love establishes the beautiful truth that at the end of the day, compromise and negotiation is needed if you are willing to make the necessary changes to see that your partner is happy. And thus, what successful relationships have in common is not the absence of inconvenience but the ability and willingness of its partners to negotiate and reach a mutual concession (compromise) whenever a problem arises.

TOPIC 5:

RELATIONSHIP WITH FRIENDS–EXTROVERT AND INTROVERT

Knowing if your partner is an extrovert or an introvert will help you better understand your partner, reduce conflicts, and greatly improve your quality of life and overall happiness. When you know that your husband or wife is an introvert, you may not be shocked when he/she turns down your offer to go to a loud, crowded bar over the weekend. And you would understand when he or she opts instead for a movie and ice cream night at home with you. Having this knowledge will help you avoid taking the rejection personally since you know it is not about you, but more about what your spouse needs to feel comfortable.

TOPIC 6:
CODEPENDENCY–UNCONDITIONAL LOVE

Codependency is a mostly negative relationship dynamic that is characterized by an excessive reliance on other people for approval and a sense of identity. Meanwhile unconditional love is affection given without any conditions, it is loving someone unselfishly and regardless of circumstance, not expecting anything in return. The major difference is that Codependency is unhealthy and Unconditional love is healthy. However, be careful that your unconditional love does not stray off its right path into the toxic way of Codependency.

TOPIC 7:
LOVE LANGUAGE–DESIRE DISCREPANCY

Love languages stem from your upbringing and childhood experiences. Perhaps while growing up, your parents routinely hugged and kissed you in the morning or late night before going to bed and told you how much they love you (Physical Touch, Words of Affirmation).

Or maybe they showed their love by always driving you personally to and from school and cheering you on each time (Acts of Service, Quality Time). Or they showered you with gifts and toys while growing up (Gifts).

Depending on whichever style your parents used overtime, you may have also adopted these love languages as your own.

TOPIC 8:
SEXUALITY–EROTIC BLUEPRINTS

An erotic blueprint refers to how a person is sexually wired – their sexual needs, responses, and desires. Your Erotic Blueprint is basically your whole erotic personality, or you could look at it as your sexual language. Your sexual language communicates what you need to get really aroused (your turn-on), your sexual preferences, how you respond sexually and what your sexual desires are. Learning and discovering yours and your partner's Erotic Blueprints can help you both expand the erotic passion you feel in your relationship and create a deeper sexual connection.

On this note, I bid you farewell. It has been a pleasure learning and understanding these life lessons with you. Cheers to your healthy, fulfilling and forever marriage ❤

WANT MORE?

ATTACHMENT THEORY

And you lived happily ever after...or at a minimum, you would if you were more interesting or attractive, or if you weren't so needy, or if you figure out what's wrong with you that makes your relationships work out badly. Maybe you've been with a partner for a long time, however, you struggle with the feeling that your companion keeps falling short and doesn't fill that hollow place in your heart.

You also suspect you are a part of the problem. They feel lonely and need companionship — not just a buddy to take a seat next to them at a movie, but a friend, a confidante, and lover to accompany them through the greatest of all adventures we call life. They regularly worry that their partner will bolt once they recognize "the real me." But sometimes they experience that their partners recognize the awesome things they do. But this isn't enough. After all, what if their performance falters?

Then there's the ever-present problem of whether or not they might really be there for them if they permit themselves to be vulnerable by trying to offer support, comfort, and reassurance. If you can relate to any of these struggles, then this ebook is for you. As a clinical psychologist, I have dealt with many people with diverse versions of these themes. Over the years, they have opened their hearts and lives to me, hoping for a tremendous alternative — and I consider that most of them realized it.

Therapy allowed them to discover the love they sought and pick companions who offered true love. With wiser choices, they created possibilities for increase and restoration. The result allowed them to revel in and nurture happier healthier relationships.

You, like a lot of my patients, may be armed with loads of information, expert advice, or a "tested formula" for success in relationships. It may come from your own family and friends, self-help books and articles, or even out of your therapist. You may have tried to fulfill the roles of Mr. or Ms. Right by socializing more or honing your online profile.

If you're already in a relationship, you may have practiced assertiveness and effective communicative skills, in addition to reminding yourself that you are worthy of love. Yet you still battle with feelings of loneliness or chronic fear of rejection.

There is a reason for this and there may be a solution. You started out studying relationships as an infant with your caretakers. I realize that's one of the clichés of psychology. However, it holds true. Your first training on how to nurture others, and on how cute you are, is based totally on the warmth, acceptance, and reassurance offered by your parents or others who took care of you. Though you cannot have been privy to this style till early life or adulthood (or perhaps it's unclear), your modern-day style might be fundamentally the same as what was nurtured in your childhood. If your early reports left you wondering about your sense of being worthy of love, scared of being rejected, or with an unquenchable thirst for reassurance, and you had poor nurturing in childhood, then you definitely experience it in this way.

It may also be the painful experiences later in life that lurked below the surface that intensified relationships. But the basic vulnerability to this attachment of partnered tension possibly developed in childhood. It's important to recognize that attachment-associated tension does not react to any obviously abusive or harmful parenting. In fact, the opposite is true. Many people with attachment-associated tension come from very loving homes. You may wonder why, then, might my attachment-related anxiety stay with me throughout my life?

To answer this, consider the endless variety of interactions you had together with your mother and father or other caretakers for the duration of your childhood, day after day, month after month, year after year. These interactions — though not all of equal weight — implicitly educate you in ways others will respond to you, teaching how worthy you are of being loved.

One critical lesson that I've discovered in doing this remedy is a little like gardening in that therapists provide people with what they want to grow. I listen, share my perceptions about their situations, offer compassion and guidance to teach them to nurture personal increase. In response, they (hopefully) discover ways to see themselves differently; reply to themselves in new, better ways; feel encouraged to chance alternatives (the unknown is always a touch scary), and learn to be different. But all of this has to show up at its own pace; it could be advocated, but it cannot be forced.

One crucial necessary detail is developing more self-cognizance. This consists of being aware of your thought, acknowledging and consciously experiencing your emotions, and knowing what makes you tick. These tasks can be tough, especially while you are facing unsightly or conflicting elements of yourself. However, they give you a higher appreciation for your struggles.

Such self-focus often allows human beings to feel an extra sense of well being and enables alterations — such as decreasing attachment-associated anxiety and the nurturing of healthier relationships. As vital as self-consciousness is, it's essential to recognize that it occurs in the context of courting yourself. And many people are too tough on themselves. Just as you'll attend to a harmed child by being nurturing, it's necessary to be compassionate towards yourself. Approaching your relationship struggles from this angle is what this ebook is about.

The explanations contained here are in an easy to understand language, and tells you how your relationship struggles were first formed, how this process made exchanges so difficult, and how these difficulties may be overcome so you can revel in a steady and lasting love.

While the main point of this ebook is to help you understand what you can do to find happiness in an intimate relationship, the ideas presented will also help you to recognize your ideal companion more easily. Sometimes, a window into your partner's world is exactly what you need to relate to his or her viewpoint, which in turn can help you nurture a healthier relationship.

The book is divided into four parts. The first helps you to understand your relationship struggles inside the context of attachment theory. Then, it opens the door to exchange through supporting you to identify limitations to nurturing your happy relationships. This explains how you can improve a steadier intimate relationship with a compassionate self-consciousness, which is basically being aware of your actions while also relating to them in an accepting and compassionate manner. "Lighting Up Your Love Life," offers suggestions for how — with a basis of compassionate self-cognizance — you can pick out a great partner and nurture a satisfied, healthful relationship.

Sign up and get your FREE copy, with a simple photo on the QR code, hoping to help you have the healthy and fulfilling life you deserve!

With Love, *THERESA MILLER*

Do not go yet; One last thing to do...

If you enjoyed this book or found it useful, I'd be very grateful if you'd post a short review on **Amazon**. Your support really does make a difference and I read all the reviews personally so I can get your feedback and make this book even better.

Thanks again for your support!

∽

© Copyright 2020 by **THERESA MILLER**
All rights reserved

Made in the USA
Las Vegas, NV
25 September 2022